THINGS WE WISH WE HAD SAID

THINGS WE WISH WE HAD SAID

REFLECTIONS OF A FATHER AND HIS SON

Tony and Bart Campolo

Authentic

10 09 08 07 06   7 6 5 4 3 2 1

First published in the USA
by Word Incorporated, Dallas, Texas.
First UK edition 1989, Word (UK) Ltd.
This edition published 2006 by Authentic Media,
9 Holdom Avenue, Bletchley, Milton Keynes, Bucks,
MK1 1QR, UK;
285 Lynnwood Avenue, Tyrone, GA 30290, USA;
OM Authentic Media India
Medchal Road, Jeedimetla Village, Secunderabad 500 055, A. P.

British Library Cataloguing in Publication Data
A catalogue record for this book is available from the British
Library.

ISBN-13: 978-1-86024-567-1
ISBN-10: 1-86024-567-6

Cover design by jaffa:design
Print Management by Adare Carwin
Printed in the UK by J.H. Haynes & Co., Sparkford

To Marty

. . . the best reason I ever had for growing up at all
B.C.

. . . the kind of daughter-in-law who makes parents
believe that marriages are made in heaven
A.C.

CONTENTS

Acknowledgements   9

Foreword to the 2006 Edition   11

Foreword   13

1. Meeting My Father's Son   15
2. How Do You Share Your Faith with Your Kid?   31
3. The Pains of Growing Up   53
4. Going Beyond the Birds and the Bees   74
5. My Friends, My Teachers, and Other Aliens   95
6. College: Where It All Comes Together or It All Falls Apart   113
7. Flying Like an Eagle When You Feel Like a Turkey   131
8. What Are You Going to Do When You Grow Up?   149
9. Doing What's Right When You Feel All Wrong   169
10. Figuring Out What Really Matters   182

Afterword   193

ACKNOWLEDGEMENTS

We are indebted to some very special people for their help in putting this book together. Without Dad's executive associate, Mary Noël Keough, and my wife, Marty, it would never have been typed. Without my mom, it would not have been edited. Pat Carroll, Sue Dahlstrom, and Sarah Thorpe also helped us turn out the manuscript. To all of these wonderful people, Dad and I say "Thank you" from the bottom of our hearts, and "thanks" to you, too, for letting us share our lives with you.

Bart Campolo

FOREWORD TO THE 2006 EDITION

As pleased as I am about this re-release of *Things We Wish We Had Said*, I must admit that reading it over again after all these years has been hard for me. The problem is not that the words themselves no longer ring true for me. On the contrary, now that my own son Roman has become a teenager, the themes and perspectives of this book make more sense to me than ever before. The difference is that now I understand my father's sections of it almost as well as my own.

No, the problem for me is that to read this book again twenty years later is to realize that I am that much closer to the end of my life and, more importantly, so is my father. Back when we wrote it, I had just graduated, and just married, and was just beginning my life as an urban minister. My father was already an established Christian leader by that time, of course, but he was still very much on the rise.

Now I am a veteran inner-city activist, with both the bank account and the cynical sense of humor to prove it, and my father has somehow become an American Christian icon, whose name and reputation follows both of us all over the world. And while he still travels and speaks and writes at a super-human pace, he has become something else that neither of us really expected. My father is an old man, closer to death than to middle age.

We talk about it all the time, in ways I could never have imagined twenty years ago and in ways that I suspect many fathers and sons never will. We talk about what his life and his accomplishments and his fame mean to other people, and to him, and to me. We talk about all the books he has written since this one, and all the books I haven't, and why. We talk about our faiths in God and our thoughts about dying, which are very different and yet eerily similar at the same time, like practically everything else about my father and me.

God, I will miss talking with my father when he dies.

My father has often told me that of all his books, many of which sold far better, *Things We Wish We Had Said* is the one which inspired the most heartfelt letters of thanks over the years. I, too, have heard from hundreds of people that our story helped them to make sense of their own, and to talk about it with their parents or their children in a better way. I hope this new edition helps even more people, especially those who have young families that are still determining their habits.

This is a book about learning to speak truly to the people who matter most—your parents and your children. Looking back, I realize how much good it did my father and me to write it, and how grateful I am for the lessons it taught us, which have only become more important to us as our time together runs short. On behalf of both of us, I hope it does you some good, too.

FOREWORD

There are four of us in the Campolo family. Peggy and I met at Eastern College when she was a freshman and I was a senior. Two years later, in June 1958, we were married. Lisa was born in 1960, followed by Bart three years later. Today, Lisa is a successful lawyer in Boston, and Bart is based in Philadelphia. He and his wife, Marty, are the founders of Kingdom Builders Supply, a non-profit-making organization helping urban churches to reach out to neighborhood youth.

Our kids were, for the most part, fun to raise. If we had it to do over again, there are a lot of things we would do the same, but there also are a lot of things we would do differently. Nobody raises kids without having some regrets, and I, personally, have a lot of them. There are things I did that I shouldn't have done, and there are things I said that I shouldn't have said. In retrospect, it is the things that I should have done and said and didn't that are far more troublesome to me. I know now that I did not deal with a lot of important stuff. Last year, Bart and I had the opportunity to share speaking responsibilities at a large youth conference. We did a lot of remembering and reflecting and shared our sometimes very different perceptions of times past. We answered some questions for the young people, but we raised even more questions for ourselves.

Bart is twenty-six years old now, and I wonder just how well we knew each other when he was growing up and how well we know each other now. I wonder just how much he understood the motivations that lay behind my actions, and I wonder how much I understood about his. Did I have any real grasp of what he was going through as he grew up? Did he have any sense of what I was thinking or that trying to be a good father was sometimes hard for me?

Looking back on those years, we sense that there was a lot concealed on both sides. That is part of what lies behind the writing of this book. In reality, Bart and I are opening up a lot of things with each other that we have not covered before. There were things I should have said to Bart that would have helped him understand me better, and, undoubtedly, there were a lot of things that he might have told me that would have helped me to do better by him as a father.

The other reason for writing this book is that I do believe there were many things that Bart and I did right during his growing up years, and I hope those things can be of some help to others who are trying to figure out the father-son thing. Perhaps our evaluation of what we did and did not do in our relationship with each other can help others to think through how they ought to raise their sons.

It also occurs to me that, in this age when so many single mothers are left with teenage sons to raise, there is much of this material that could be useful to them. Single mothers may get some help in understanding what a son needs from a father and what a father ought to be giving to his son. A knowledge of what is missing is required before a single mother can consider how to compensate for a father who isn't there.

A book like this one could be written by my daughter and me, or, for that matter, by my son and his mother, but this time it's Bart and me. If at times we seem to leave Peggy and Lisa out of it, it's only because we don't presume to speak for them. Bart and I hope that what we have to say to each other in these letters will prove useful to anyone who is trying to be a good parent to a boy who is trying to become an adult—and we also hope that this book will be of help to young people who have to work at both growing up *and* figuring out their parents at the same time.

Tony Campolo

ONE

MEETING MY FATHER'S SON

Dear Dad,

You are an incredibly tough act to follow. Whenever I compare myself to you, I come out the loser, Dad, and yet, more and more as I get older, I can't stop myself from doing it all the same.

I think you are a great father. Having said that, though, I still need to answer the question of what it means to be your son. I have to answer it for myself, the same way you had to answer it about your father and he had to answer it about his. You may not be "Tony Campolo, Christian leader" to me, but you are my dad, and that is enough for anyone to come to terms with. It's not a matter of what you did right or what you did wrong in raising me as much as it's the standard you set just by being who you are.

Perhaps the best way I can describe it to you is to use our basketball games as an example, because for me those games have always reflected our relationship and personalities better than anything else. From the very first time you took me down to the gym at Eastern College to teach me how to shoot, I realized that basketball was something you really cared about. It was fun, to be sure, but it was also important to you that I learn to play the game the right way, and because it was important to you, it became important to me as well, right from the start. After that, I spent a lot of time with a basketball in my hands, practicing the fundamentals and imagining myself as a star player with you in the stands cheering me on. Fortunately, I had some natural ability to go along with my intense desire to please you, and by the time I was ten years old I was good enough to play with you in the pick-up games you were always finding wherever we happened to be.

It was a hustle, really, except that we didn't play people for money. We would walk onto the court as though we had never seen one before and begin to shoot the ball awkwardly, cheering wildly whenever we managed to hit the rim. The college guys at the other end of the court would watch our act for a while and then go on with their game. They were always surprised when you walked over and asked them if they wanted to take us on, and nine times out of ten they declined, not wanting to show up a klutzy father in front of his adoring son. Somehow, though, you usually managed to embarrass them into it. "What's the matter?" you'd jeer."Are you guys afraid you can't keep up with an old man and a little kid?" They'd go easy on us at first, so that by the time they figured out how good we really were, we usually had a pretty big lead. Then they'd bear down on us, but most times it was a case of too little too late.

I always got a kick out of those games; even though my job was mainly to throw the ball to you and watch you beat both of the other guys single-handed. Oh, I'd shoot a few baskets to keep them honest, but it was definitely your show. Even when they were better, we usually won anyway because you simply refused to let us lose. I've seen a lot of basketball players, Dad, but I've never seen anyone as hard-nosed as you are in a game. You would dive after loose balls, smash into guys twice your size, and run over anyone who got in your way. I asked you about it once, and you told me that when you were growing up in the city, the playground courts were always crowded with guys waiting to play. The team that won kept playing while the losers went to the end of the line, so everyone hated to lose. Kids in the city play basketball for blood. You had to be tough, you told me, and after watching you play, I didn't doubt it.

Later on, we began to play against each other, one-on-one, and you always won. I got bigger and stronger and more skillful every year, but you won anyway, even after I had clearly become the better player. I could beat players who could in turn beat you, but somehow that never translated when we matched up together. No matter how big a lead I managed to build, you always caught me in the end with a clutch steal or an impossible shot.

"You'll never beat me," you used to rib me between baskets, "because you're not tough enough. You don't want it bad enough. Face it, kid, you're soft."

You were kidding, of course, but we both knew that you were right, too. I was not tough. I'm still not tough. Even though I made the varsity team like you had, I was always a finesse player, relying on my skills and shying away from heavy contact. I was talented enough, but I lacked the "killer instinct" that makes a talented player a winner. You, however, were a scrapper without great height or dazzling speed and without my ball-handling abilities, but you were armed with an aggressiveness I'll never have.

One time, at a Bible conference where you were speaking, I thought I was finally going to beat you. We were in a five-on-five game that day, but guarding each other made it one-on-one between us, and I was outdoing you in a big way at both ends of the court. Toward the end, we started really banging each other around, both of us intent on winning the game. We were having fun, but the other players probably thought we were trying to kill each other (you certainly weren't "turning the other cheek" the way you had preached about that morning!). On the last point, I took the ball and drove hard for the winning basket. You appeared out of nowhere and knocked both me and the ball to the ground. You not only blocked my shot, you bloodied my nose as well. The other men looked embarrassed as I got up, but you and I just laughed. "You should know better than to try something like that, kid," you said with a sly grin, and the game went on. My team lost—again.

I never could win. I had to wait until age slowed you down before I ever took a game from you, and when it finally happened, we both knew that it wasn't really me who had beaten you after all. Even when I won, I lost. That's the way it is for me with you. I have every advantage, but you win on character. And if, perchance, you don't, well, anyone can see that I have all the advantages. It's never a real victory! And make no mistake—I'm not just thinking about basketball anymore. It's the way our lives are.

You see, I know all about your life. I know because I remember all those stories you told me about growing up on the streets of West Philadelphia, the youngest son of an immigrant family too poor to buy you your opportunities. I know that you got the same toy truck three Christmases in a row, except that every year it was painted a different color so you'd think it was new. (Frankly, I've always wondered how such an intelligent man could have been such a stupid kid.) I know that you lived in a tiny row house with rooms the size of closets—you even showed me the house once. I know about fighting to keep from being robbed . . . about having to share the weekly bottle of soda pop with your two older sisters . . . about hitchhiking because you didn't have bus fare . . . and I know your father died partly because he was too poor to have a good doctor until it was too late.

I also know that you worked for your family as a kid and gave the money you earned to your parents. I know that you worked your way through college, too, and then seminary. Even if you hadn't told me about it all yourself, I would still know because Mom-Mom Campolo told those same stories about you, over and over again. She was so proud of you and of what you had accomplished, and she wanted me to be proud, too. She wanted me to understand that it is a great thing to come from a poor Italian family in the inner city and earn a Ph.D. and become a college professor and a famous preacher as well. She wanted me to see you as a great man, not because of your gifts and abilities, but because you overcame so many obstacles to become a scholar and a servant of God by the sheer force of your own will. "Your father," she'd tell me, "went over the top for Jesus."

I guess every kid has heard a slew of those often-repeated when-I-was-your-age stories. They are our parents' way of letting us know that no matter what we happen to be going through at the time, they had it worse. They are a kind of oral tradition, too, a family history that's passed down from one generation to the next. I always liked listening to those stories because they told me that I was part of a larger tradition. Mom-Mom Campolo told them all the time, but Grandmom and Grandpop Davidson waited to be asked, I think because they thought I would be bored. On the contrary, I love knowing about who and where we come from as a family, except when I know you're using one of those when-I-was-your-age stories to manipulate me into doing something.

To a well-heeled suburban kid like me, though, being poor didn't always sound all that horrible. The way you described it, your childhood seemed like one adventure after another—a constant battle against anything that tried to hold you back. "We were poor," you'd say, "but boy, did we know how to have fun." I can remember thinking that stickball in the streets sounded a whole lot more exciting than my Little League with all its fancy uniforms and coaches and practice sessions, and that hitching across the city on your own sounded a whole lot better than getting driven to school in Mom's station wagon. My life was surely more comfortable than yours, but it was just as surely more boring, too. Besides, you made it very clear to me that it was the hardships you had to overcome, the sacrifices you had to make, and especially the hard work you had to do that made you into the person you are today. I could tell you were proud of your childhood. You had to fight to survive, you said, and it made a man out of you.

So now, after all of the years of wondering, I must finally ask you the obvious question: Why did you let me grow up without all of those things that made such a difference in your life? How could you raise me in the lap of luxury and expect me to develop character, when you had already fought all of my character-building battles for me when you were becoming a man? Didn't it occur to you that by sparing me from the hardships, the sacrifices, the hard work, and the fights you were robbing me of the chance to become the kind of man you are?

Take a good look at me. What have I accomplished? What have I achieved? I'm a white, Anglo-Saxon, Protestant male raised by two highly educated parents in an affluent suburban community in the richest country in the world. I've never been beaten, hungry, discriminated against, or too poor for anything, including an Ivy League education. I worked at summer jobs when I was in school, of course, but the money I earned was my own, to buy things I wanted, because you bought everything I needed. You would be hard pressed to find anyone in the world who has had any more advantages than I have had. The problem is that I didn't do anything to earn all those things, except manage to be born in the right place at the right time. You are the one who earned it, not me. Because of that, you know a lot of things about yourself that I'll never be able to know about myself. You know that you're tough and that you have character. You know that you can make a way for yourself and that you deserve to be where you are in the world. Those are important things, Dad.

I remember during the 1988 election, they said that George Bush was "someone who was born on third base and thought he'd hit a triple." I don't know about George Bush, but I'm well aware that I didn't overcome anything to put myself where I am. I never had that chance.

So how can I measure up to you, Dad? How can I accomplish anything that will compare to your Horatio Alger rags-to-riches story? We both know the answer to those questions: I can't. The game was over before it started. I have begun to understand why so many children of successful people rebel against their parents' value system altogether: they know that they can't make it work. When you start at the top, there really isn't any direction you can go except down. Maybe that sounds like self-pity to you, but surely there's some truth to it. You never had to think about that, of course, because your situation was precisely the opposite of mine—you had nowhere to go but up. You weren't born on third base, or even on second. Consequently, there was no pressure on you to achieve any particular degree of success. By the time you were graduated from high school, you had already gone farther than your parents ever could have dreamed of going themselves. You could take chances with your life, secure in the knowledge that wherever you ended up you were already a winner. You had nothing to lose and everything to gain, whereas my situation is exactly the reverse.

You see, Dad, it's not just that I started out with so much. The rules of the game have changed as well.

For the first time in history, economists tell us, the generation presently coming of age cannot expect to achieve a higher standard of living than their parents. Certainly there are more and better opportunities than ever before, but there's also more competition as well. There are more people, for one thing. The rewards of success are higher than ever, but then so is the price. Take education, for example. I've always felt guilty that you put me through college because I know that you worked yourself through without any help from your parents. But even if I had tried to work my way through school, how could I have earned enough to pay for a private education? It's more than I make in a year now, working full time. (If college students could make that much a year in part-time jobs, they might wonder if it made sense to be in college in the first place or if they wouldn't be better off making careers out of whatever it was they were already doing so successfully.) The point is that things are different now from what they were when you were my age. The odds are stacked even more heavily against a kid on his own than they were only ten years ago, let alone twenty-five. Yet even knowing all that doesn't really quell my self-doubts, because somehow I sense you could find a way to make it today if you had to, and somehow I worry that I wouldn't have been able to do the same if I had been in your shoes during the fifties.

I think that kind of feeling is often a big factor in why kids rebel against their parents. Convinced that they will lose if they play "the game" and try to live up to their parents' standard of success, they opt not to try at all. They look for another game, another way to establish themselves in the world. Unfortunately that isn't always as easy as it seems because of the way heredity can limit options.

Years ago, I watched an interview with Joe Frazier, the heavyweight boxing champion of the world at the time. His son, Marvis, was no more than ten years old, and I remember Joe telling the interviewer that he did not want Marvis to become a boxer. "He should be a doctor or a lawyer or something like that, where you use your head for something other than getting hit," Joe said earnestly. I thought it was great that he wasn't pressuring his son to follow in his footsteps, because clearly Joe's shoes would be nearly impossible to fill. But I wasn't surprised eight years later to find Marvis Frazier boxing professionally on television. Whether he liked it or not, Marvis Frazier had the body of a boxer, just like his dad. Besides, he had practically been raised in Joe's North Philadelphia gym, surrounded by other fighters. That he would become a boxer was almost inevitable. He wasn't as good as his dad though, and something he said after he lost the fight badly summed up the tragedy of that fact: "I'm not my dad," he said, "but I'm going to keep boxing anyway because that's what I do best."

I can relate to that one myself, because all of the things I do best are the things you do best as well. You do them better than I do, of course, but they are still my strengths. What makes it worse for me is that, as a Christian, I feel bound to utilize my gifts and abilities as best I can for the Kingdom of God—even though that means leaving myself open to comparison with you. I've tried doing a lot of other things, but I've always come back to speaking and teaching because, for better or for worse, those are the things I am gifted to do, just like you. But you're more than just gifted as a speaker. You're aggressive, the same way you were in basketball. To other people it may seem as though you're talking off the top of your head (and I'll just skip the obvious jokes, because I inherited your pitiful hair genes along with some of the good ones), but I know how much work goes into those sermons. I've watched you study for hours to master a difficult idea just so you can make it seem easy to the people you'll explain it to later. There are no easy ways to find new things to say or new ways to say old things, but you keep doing it year after year. You push yourself hard before you even stand up to speak, let alone once you're doing your thing. You know how to "read" audiences, too, with a wisdom that comes from having preached a hundred times to every kind of group as you worked your way up the ladder to become a top speaker. You are a gifted speaker, Dad, but you are a workman as well.

I'm a speaker, too, but I didn't have to work very hard to become one. I had you as an example and as a teacher, for one thing, which is a serious head start. I also have your last name as well, which helps more than you can imagine. People are always giving me opportunities to speak, sometimes at places where you had to wait twenty years to win a hearing, simply because I'm your son. I don't try to kid myself that I've earned my chances, and I don't pretend that I have the same drive and ability that keeps you on top of the game. I do my very best—make no mistake about that—but, like Marvis Frazier, I have to admit that I'm not my dad, even though speaking is what I do best. The chances come because of whose son I am.

Think about this book that I'm writing at the tender age of twenty-six. Neither of us is foolish enough to think that anyone would publish my writing if my name were Bart Smith. It's you, Dad. We both know that. Of course, I take those opportunities just the same, and I put everything I have into making the most of them. I don't like admitting it sometimes, but the way I've resolved all of this speaking stuff is to treat being your son and having your last name the same way I would treat any other spiritual gift: as something to be used to serve God and his people. So many doors open for me because of you that I seldom feel like I've earned my position, but I'm ready and willing to trade that sense of accomplishment for the opportunity to share the Gospel and the chance to challenge people to live their lives for the love of God and the love of his people. I may not say things as well as you do, but that has nothing to do with what the Holy Spirit can or cannot do through me, so I've learned to depend on God and not worry about everything else. It may be a rationalization, but as long as I can preach the Gospel, organize ministries in the inner city, and invite young people to commit themselves to Christian service, it's a rationalization with which I can live.

But that still doesn't resolve the larger issue between you and me. Maybe nothing really can. You didn't choose your environment, and neither did I. Your parents weren't able to give you all of the things they'd have liked to have given you, and you became a fine man. You gave me everything, but even as you gave it, you took something away from me that I know you wouldn't want taken from you. You kept me from making it on my own. Perhaps I sound like the most horribly ungrateful person you could ever imagine, but I'm counting on you to know better than that. The most important thing in the world is love, and we both had plenty of that growing up. It's just that when I look at the world around me and see all of the suffering and need, I feel guilty about everything I've received. More and more I get angry when people talk about prosperity as though it were a reward for godliness, because I know that, in my case, it has a lot more to do with family background and because most of the finest Christians I know are poor. They love and depend on God in ways I'll never understand, and it offends me to hear people suggest otherwise in order to justify their own wealth or the way they spend it.

No words in all the world frighten me like those of Jesus: "From everyone who has been given much, much will be demanded; and from the one who has been entrusted with much, much more will be asked" (Luke 12:48). That verse haunts me through all of this, and it may be why I sometimes long for someone else's beginning. For God has much to say to those to whom he has given talents, wealth, education, opportunities, and, above all, grace. In this country, we often fail to listen, but one day we'll have no choice. When I was a boy, the worst thing in the world wasn't to anger you, Dad, but to disappoint you. I feel the same way about my Heavenly Father. I don't fear for my salvation, but I worry about what I'll say when I stand before God and must tell him what I did with everything he gave me. Sometimes it keeps me up at night. I worry about our entire nation and especially about American Christians, and I wonder what account we'll offer for our lifestyles of excess while our brothers and sisters went hungry and died. I think the Day of Judgment may not be our favorite part of eternity, for what could be more unhappy than to have disappointed the most wonderful Loved One we'll ever have by wasting his treasures and allowing his children to suffer? There is grace, to be sure, and there is forgiveness, but what account will we ever give, as individuals and as a nation, if we do not begin to listen to the voice of God?

As for me, I worry about my character as well, and I fear that in missing the struggles that you overcame, I've also missed the chance to become strong. You're a fine man,

Dad, and I'm very grateful for that—I just wonder sometimes how I'm ever going to become the same kind of man
myself.

Love,

Bart

*   *   *   *

Dear Bart,

If, according to Freud, the resolution of the Oedipus complex
is brought about because a boy makes a positive identification
with his father, then you were well on your way to resolving
that complex in your preadolescent years. You always made
me aware of your admiration for me, even when you were a
little kid.

When you were about nine years old, the whole family went
along with me to a speaking engagement at a small rural
church. As we drove into the parking lot of the church, we saw
only four cars, indicating that the church would be far from
filled. Sizing up the situation, you exclaimed, "Dad! This is a
disgrace! Hardly anybody has come to hear you speak—and
you're so famous!"

Lisa, who has always had a knack for seeing things as they
really are, responded, "Well, Bart, if he's so famous, where are
all the people?"

You, in your usual cavalier manner, answered, "Knock it off,
Lisa—it's pretty tough being famous when nobody knows
who you are!"

You were always like that. Your mind was made up about
your dad, and you weren't about to be confused with the
facts. You gave me what I'm sure almost every father wants
from his son—admiration. I must say, however, that at times
I've felt that your admiration was undeserved and at other
times frightening. The hero worship that a son can give a
father sometimes ignores many flaws and failures. You certainly were blinded to many of my failures and made me out

to be bigger than life. Let me note some things you should consider.

In my drive for success, I worked too hard and too long and too often exhausted myself physically. Consequently, I was often irritable and short with people. You and Lisa were usually spared my nastiness, but Mom on too many occasions had to bear the brunt of how I felt. I don't know how much of that unfair meanness toward Mom you observed. I know that you saw some. I look back on my behavior at such times with shame and feel guilt. The Lord never willed for me to work so long and hard as to be that strung out.

Jesus himself set the example for recognizing the limits of physical endurance and for stopping even godly service before exhaustion could lead to falling into sinful behavior. In Matthew 8:16–18, we read about his ministering to people. When he became exhausted, he told his disciples that he was worn out and that it was time for him to stop and to pull himself together. The disciples weren't very understanding, and they pressed him by saying that there were scores of people who were still waiting to be healed and served. Jesus asserted himself at that point and demanded to be put into a boat and taken to the other side of the Sea of Galilee.

Jesus knew how to say when enough was enough—but, then, he *was* the Messiah, while some of the rest of us only have messiah *complexes*. We act as though we should never stop working as long as there are people out there asking for our help. We're motivated more out of egotism than love, and we kid ourselves if we pretend otherwise. We end up pushing too hard and then taking it out on those who are closest to us, who love us, and who have gotten far less of our time than they had a right to expect.

As you admire ambition, take a second look at it in my life. I think that there will be a lot about my ambition and what it has done to those I love—and to me—that is deserving of your criticism.

I think that my ambition was in large measure built into me by my poor Italian parents. My mother was a first-generation American, and my dad immigrated here as a boy. They bought into the American Dream in a much bigger way than most people who accept it as their inheritance. My parents saw being American not as a given, but rather as something to be achieved. In such a family, I grew up as a marginal person, not fully belonging to the "American" way of life, but also not having any sense of real at-homeness in the Italian subculture of my extended family. People like me work desperately to be accepted, and part of my drive, I am sure, stems from the sense that my personal achievements somehow earn me a place in the dominant culture. This kind of a background made me ambitious, but it also conditioned me to live on tiptoe for most of my life. I need to be accepted.

You may not have the kind of drive that sometimes goes with being a first-generation ethnic, but there is a positive side to not having it that I don't want you to ignore or take for granted. You are so much more relaxed about life. You enjoy life more. You seem to be able to stop and smell the roses. You come across as someone who knows that he belongs and does-n't have to "show off" to earn a place in this world. Count your blessings, kid.

I concur with your assessment that you may not have that inner sense of drivenness to do as much as I feel driven to do, but don't be so sure that your talent will not be enough to make you a much greater achiever. In your letter, you mentioned what you learned from me on the basketball court—but do you remember that, even without my knock-down-sock-it-to-'em style, you were a good high-school basketball player?

In your very first regular-season game as a varsity basketball player, you came off the bench and scored a team-high nineteen points to lead your team to victory. Your smooth moves and natural style led to an array of floating jump shots that had the fans on their feet. You may not have been a blood-and-guts guy under the boards, but on that day, your sheer talent made your team a winner. You never did become the star player I thought you could have been, but I always admired the way you kept things in perspective. There's something wrong with wanting to be a winner at all costs.

It's true that I've had to work my head off to overcome some of the limitations of my background, but that doesn't mean that what I produce is better than what you produce. For instance, anybody who reads this book will become aware of the fact that you are a good writer. You may not have had to work very hard to become a good writer, and you probably would be an even better writer if you drove yourself a little harder, but your talent enables you to accomplish much, much more than I could have ever dreamed of doing at your age. You write better than I do already. It is only that I have more life experiences to draw from that keeps me in the same league with you.

Bart, you often have heard me say that *being* is more important than *doing*. I sometimes preach a sermon that strongly declares that what a person *is* is more important than what a person *does*. As far as I'm concerned, you, more than anyone else I know, validate that sermon. You have learned how to *be*, and this is more important than learning how to do.

Sometimes I'm so busy in programs and projects that I forget people. Too often, those who work in sacrificial commitment to the visions of ministry that I've given them tell me how their feelings have been hurt because of my inattentiveness to them as persons. I'm always crushed when my failure to feel for people like I should is pointed out to me, and I long to be a more sensitive person. Caring for people is one area in which I wish I were like you. I admire you for your relationships and your awareness of how other people are feeling.

A good example of what I'm talking about comes to mind as I remember the summer of 1985. I had asked one of my friends, Jim Burns, who was then director of youth ministries at South Coast Community Church in Newport Beach, California, to take you on as an intern. In previous years, you had chosen to work in my youth programs among the poor kids of Philadelphia. That year, though, I thought that the time had come for you to recognize that rich kids have their problems, too. So Jim set it up for you to join him as a summer intern to work with the church young people. My friend was well aware that you didn't need any "up front" experience as a speaker, so he minimized that particular role for you in your work with him. Instead, your job was to address the personal, spiritual, and psychological needs of the kids in the youth group as a support person and counselor.

Jim's reports to me at the end of that summer were filled with superlatives. He told me how your ability to empathize with teenagers made them eager to accept you as their friend, how your concern for them as individuals made you ever ready to provide long hours of listening for them. Jim talked glowingly about the kind of person you were and of the way in which you related to people who hurt. I was proud of you.

When I heard about your ministry out there in Newport Beach, I knew for sure that you had something that was far more precious than drive in your keen sensitivity for people. Sometimes those of us who have plans to change the world fail to feel for the needs of individuals who are hurting. Sometimes we're blind to the emotional needs of those who are staring us in the face. Not so with you, Bart! Not so with you!

There was, however, something that you mentioned about your upbringing in your letter which bothered me, and that was your questioning me about having raised you in the suburbs. The suburbs are "dangerous" places for kids, and your reflections on growing up there have me second-guessing and wondering what would have been best for you.

Suburbs are, for the most part, plastic enclaves where kids can grow up separated from the realities that torture most of the world. Poverty is unknown. The old and the decrepit are carefully removed. The ugly side of life remains out of sight. Pimps, whores, and street people all live "downtown." Suburban kids live in a never-never land of narcissistic self-indulgence where nothing is ever asked of them except that they be constantly happy. Psychologists, like Harvard's Robert Coles, point out that kids in such environments lack any real purpose for living and often become depressed and bored with life because they can find no significant reason for their existence.

I tried to keep you from these maladies of suburban life by regularly taking you to places where there was suffering and involving you in work that would serve the needs of the poor. Remember when I took you with me up to Wilkes-Barre, Pennsylvania, after a flood had devastated that city? Do you remember working side by side with me as we shoveled mud out of basements and cleaned up homes for desperate people?

Remember our trips to Haiti and the Dominican Republic, where you were forced to look on the pain of the poor of the Third World? Remember being taken by Mom to visit elderly shut-ins who were lonely and sad? We tried to compensate for your "impoverished" life in the suburbs, but I still think you're right. It wasn't enough to overcome all that the suburbs do to kids.

Now you have Kingdom Builders Supply, your own inner-city mission outreach program. You'll be recruiting scores of college kids who have grown up in suburbia to come and join you in your ministry. You and these collegians will be working out of inner-city churches to reach some of the most oppressed and disadvantaged kids of America. I know that the parents of these college kids will be telling you of their concerns regarding the safety of their children in the city. They will be worried about what might happen in the city to suburban-bred young people who are in no way streetwise, and they are right to be concerned, because there is real danger on the city streets.

If those parents could understand what I've been talking about here, they would be even more concerned about what will happen to their children if they *don't* come to work with you and simply live out their lives in the "dangerous" suburbs. These parents should be worried about children who never escape from the stifling world of the "good life," where all appears to be well, but really isn't. They ought to be asking what will happen to kids who live where there is nothing at all about which to concern themselves—except for their own personal happiness. Parents ought to be begging you to take their children on as volunteers instead of just worrying about their safety.

Your letter shows me that you understand the liabilities of suburban living all too well. Maybe in your ministry you can make others understand this, too.

Love,

Dad

TWO

HOW DO YOU SHARE YOUR FAITH WITH YOUR KID?

Dear Bart,

One of the most difficult problems for any Christian father is how to tell his kids about Christ and lead them into a personal relationship with him. This was no less of a problem for a father who happened to be on the preaching circuit as a speaker for evangelical gatherings. As a matter of fact, Bart, I sometimes felt that it was harder for me to talk to you about a vital personal faith in Christ because I was a preacher. I felt that way for a number of good reasons.

First, there was always the concern that, growing up in a Christian home and having the gospel thrown at you so many times and in so many ways, you might become indifferent to it all. I was afraid that hearing the message of Christ over and over again might keep you from taking it seriously. I feared that daily exposure might inoculate you with Christianity and render you immune to the real disease. This was a real possibility. I've seen a good number of kids from Christian families (and not just preachers' families) who seemed to have developed the capacity to turn off the claims of Christ because of the years of practice they got in doing it as they grew up. Sometimes a guy like you can be told something so many times that he just doesn't hear it anymore. Overexposure can be a real turnoff, and I always harbored the fear that you might have been overexposed.

In addition to the fact that you heard me articulate the way of salvation from the pulpit on innumerable occasions, I made special efforts to outline the gospel story for you on a one-to-one basis.

You may not remember this, but once I took you with me to a men's Bible conference at Keuka College in upper New York State. After a lot of prayerful preparation, during which I asked God to give me the right words to say to you, we started out on the five-hour drive to the conference. I had planned for us to have this long time together so that I could talk to you in an unrushed and relaxed manner. I figured that, during the trip, I could get the discussion going in a casual way, entertain questions, and then resolve the matter of your making a decision for Christ.

Everything started out as I had hoped that it would. We got to discussing who Jesus was and is and what being a Christian is all about. You asked questions and engaged in a lively exchange with me for more than an hour.

The one thing I did not do was to press you to make a decision. Both of us now agree that it is not enough for a person to believe in what Jesus did on the cross and what he is presently doing in the world. We know that, in addition to believing the right things, a person must make a decision to allow the resurrected Jesus to be *Lord*. That involves a commitment to do what Jesus would do if he were in your place and facing your options. Being a Christian requires a commitment to obey the will of God as revealed in Scripture and as discovered through both prayer and the help of other Christians in the church.

I guess I failed to press you to make a decision that day because the way you talked to me led me to believe that you had already made your commitment to Christ. Looking back on it now, I think that I made a mistake at that point. Too often we take things for granted when talking with loved ones—particularly those in our own family.

I am convinced that when a person believes in what Christ accomplished through his death and resurrection and chooses to surrender fully to the will of God, such a person will be born again. By that I mean that the presence of Christ will be "felt." With full surrender comes the consciousness that Christ is close at hand and even within. It's like being aware of a friend who is ever present. It's the good feeling that he is always there for you to lean on for help and direction. I wanted you to have that kind of relationship with Christ. I wanted you to know the aliveness that comes from being in Christ and from having Christ in you. I suppose I should have pressed you that day to yield yourself to Christ's lordship; but I didn't. Once again, my fear was of putting you on some kind of spiritual overload that might set off a negative reaction that would have moved you away from Christianity.

Second, I often wondered if seeing the inconsistencies between what I preached and what I practiced would make you cynical about my own professions of Christianity and even about the gospel itself. I don't think any of us are as good as the message we preach. I know that the Christ I declare is much more than can be seen in the way I live from day to day. As best I can, I try to let my listeners know that, in this respect, I am like the Apostle Paul who wrote: "I press toward the mark for the prize of the high calling of God in Christ Jesus" (Philippians 3:14). I try not to pretend that I'm an actualized or completed Christian. Instead, I endeavor to communicate the fact that I am still very much involved in the process of being transformed into the likeness of Christ and to invite those who listen to join me in the lifelong struggle to overcome the darkness that is in all of us.

Regardless of my qualifying statements, I think you expected more of me, and I worried that my failure to live up to what I called for from the pulpit (for people to become) would lead you to think that Christian leaders were phonies whose messages were not to be taken seriously.

The point at which I was most concerned was in respect to my lifestyle. There is no question in my mind that being a Christian requires a commitment to a radical lifestyle that I myself have failed to approximate. Along with Deitrich Bonhoeffer, I believe that "When Jesus calls a man, he bids him come and die." But if there's anything I haven't done, it is to die to the affluent American lifestyle.

On the basis of my preaching, some people are led to think that I live in a hovel and never spend any money on worldly pleasures. I've declared that Christians ought to live simply so that others might simply live. I've pointed out in sermon after sermon that there's something drastically wrong when Christians think that they can be followers of Jesus, yet ignore what he tells the rich to do about the poor and the oppressed of the world. After all the rationalizations for an affluent lifestyle are given, all of us must face what is written in 1 John 3:17–18.

> But whoso hath this world's good, and seeth his brother have need, and shutteth up his bowels of compassion from him, how dwelleth the love of God in him? My little children, let us not love in word, neither in tongue; but in deed and truth.

There is no way of escaping the almost six hundred passages in the Bible that call us to work out our commitment to God by sacrificially serving the poor with the resources he has placed in our hands. If there is anything that has marked my preaching, it has been the declaration that Christians should look and act more like Francis of Assisi and Mother Teresa. I don't believe that good works for the poor will save us, but I do believe that being a Christian is having your heart broken by the things that break the heart of Jesus and that having the mind of Christ (Philippians 2:5) means we will inevitably think like he would think and act like he would act—particularly toward the downtrodden people who cross our paths.

The excuse I usually give to those who inquire about my lifestyle is that my wife does not agree with me as to how we ought to live. The simple lifestyle principles are not part of what she considers to be essential to Christianity. I tell myself that I've made concessions to her as part of maintaining a good marriage. There is some truth to this argument.

I think you know me well enough to know that if I had had my way, I certainly would have opted for living in the inner city where I could have had direct contact with the urban poor. I grew up among the poor and went to school with oppressed minority people, and I identify with their plight. The cries of those inner-city people who receive only the short end of society's opportunities are very much a part of what I have carried to the middle-class audiences to whom I speak.

While it is true that where we live is in large measure determined by the fact that Mom did not and does not feel called to
live among the poor, I know you are aware that, in a host of
ways, I've bought into a great deal of the affluent lifestyle quite
apart from her influence. I may drive an old car, I may not
spend a lot of money on clothes, and I shy away from the sym-
bols of wealth and status which are so much a part of
American bourgeois society. Nevertheless, I have my own particular splurges with which you are all-too-well acquainted.
For instance, I love to travel and end up spending more than a
frugal Christian should on vacations. Also, when I travel in
connection with my speaking engagements, I usually end up
being entertained in first-class ways. Staying at the best hotels
is not exactly what the people who hear me preach think of me
as doing. I can live high while spending very little because
those who invite me to speak pay the bills. I sometimes feel a
bit uncomfortable about all of this, but not enough to put my
foot down and demand more simple living.

Perhaps the point at which I feel the greatest discomfort is
when people visit our home. We bought the house at a price that
in today's market would be a fantastic bargain, and we chose to
buy it because it was located within walking distance of my
office and in a very safe neighborhood. Since my work was
going to keep me on the road so much of the time, I agreed with
Mom that she should live in a safe community. It wouldn't have
been fair to ask her to live in a place where she felt she didn't
belong, especially when I wouldn't be there much of the time.

Yet, when all the pros and cons have been given, I still have
a sense of guilt about having such a lovely (and now expensive) house. There's much more room in it than we use, and it
costs too much to maintain it. When I think of people squeezed
into huts in Haiti or into ghetto tenements, it doesn't seem fair
that I should have so much extra space. From time to time
we've helped out students by having them live with us, but all
in all I feel uneasy about all the room we have and really do
not share.

In the end, it is probably having been socialized into loving
privacy that has conditioned my housing habits. In this, I share
with all Americans the tendency to have more housing space

than I need. Bart, I know you share this uneasiness of mine, and I hope that the way Mom and I have lived has not led you to think me hypocritical.

Third, I've worried about how much my failure to conduct regular family devotions could have adversely influenced your willingness to become a Christian. From time to time, I initiated special times for Bible reading and prayer, but it was hard for me to maintain consistency in these spiritual disciplines since my personal schedule was so helter-skelter. With evening meetings on more weekdays than not, I wasn't home at suppertime often enough to make a relaxed devotional time a regular part of our family life. Breakfast time always seemed to be too filled with anxious anticipation to permit me to take time for sacred reflection, I wish now that I had put more creative energy and time into planning family devotions. I suppose if I had worked at it, or even if I had been more demanding, I could have made it work—but I didn't. I sensed resistance and just gave up.

In those early days of your life, Mom wasn't on the kind of spiritual wavelength that would have led her to view family devotions as being of great significance. I know because she says so herself, and if she had it to do over again, things would be different. Since her Christian experience a few years ago, she has put us all to shame with her spiritual concerns. Back then, however, Mom just didn't see the need for family devotions, and I never made it a bone of contention between us.

Even if my Christian commitment failed to compel me to make regular devotions a part of our lives, my knowledge of sociology should have caused me to make them a family ritual. You have heard me give numerous lectures on the positive influences that rituals can have on individuals and particularly on children. Rituals (like family devotions) have been proven to be a primary factor in building loyalty and cohesiveness among family members. "The family that prays together stays together" is not simply a cliché; it is an articulation of a sound sociological principle.

Ever since sociologist Emile Durkheim first outlined the role that rituals can have in building group solidarity and inculcating values into children, people in my discipline have known that practices like regular family devotions are more important in Christian education than all of the Sunday school lessons that could ever be taught. I'm sure that the reason Jesus instituted Holy Communion was to turn every meal into a ritual that would renew the memory of his death and resurrection and revitalize the faith of his disciples. I do not think that his command that we should remember his death and resurrection whenever we eat or drink until he comes again was meant to be something occasionally observed at church worship services. Consider exactly what he said when he instituted this sacrament/ordinance:

> And when he had given thanks, he brake it, and said, Take, eat: this is my body, which is broken for you: this do in remembrance of me. After the same manner also he took the cup, when he had supped, saying, "This cup is the new testament in my blood: this do ye, as oft as ye drink it, in remembrance of me."
>
> *1 Corinthians 11:24–25*

Jesus distinctly wanted to make every meal into a ritual in which his saving work for us would be remembered. It seems to me that Jesus wanted every meal to be a devotional time. I believe that if we followed what I read as his mandate on this, our lives would be consistently holier and our tendencies to fail or waver spiritually would be dramatically diminished.

Both my understanding of sociology and my reading of the Bible should have compelled me to treat the matter of having family devotions on a daily basis with a sense of urgency. It seems to me that parents who fail in this Christian discipline ought not to be surprised if their children fail to become committed to Christ as they grow older. I know that I should have been a better father in this respect, particularly in the face of the indifference Mom had to such matters back then. Forgive me.

Last of all, Bart, I think that I may have failed you by not letting you know about my own doubts and times of spiritual dryness. It's difficult for any parent to know what to do about these matters. On the one hand, I think it's a mistake to communicate to kids that Christians experience an uninterrupted life of confident faith and spiritual joy. For all who follow Christ, there are times of painful depression and times of questioning. Jesus himself had such times. As I read about his prayer in Gethsemane, I am convinced that at that point in his life he was going through such a "down time" that he struggled with what being an obedient Son of God was all about. In Matthew 26:37–39, we read:

> And he took with him Peter and the two sons of Zebedee, and began to be sorrowful and very heavy. Then saith he unto them, "My soul is exceeding sorrowful, even unto death: tarry ye here, and watch with me. And he went a little further, and fell on his face, and prayed, saying, O my Father, if it be possible, let this cup pass from me: nevertheless not as I will, but as thou wilt."

On the cross, as he bore the sins of the world, Jesus experienced doubts and cried out to his father: "My God, my God, why hast thou forsaken me?" (Matthew 27:46). I'm sure that in his cry to his father he was using the opening words of Psalm 22, and, like the Psalmist, overcame those torturous doubts in a way that enabled him to declare triumphantly to the world, "It is finished!" Throughout the entire passion story, however, I see a Savior who was willing to display his doubts and depressing struggles. He makes it clear that one need not be in sin to fall into such painful states of being. His example makes it easier for me to work through my spiritual down times and doubts and to grasp that living out the will of God is not some kind of easy joyride without any depressions. Perhaps I should have tried to do for you what Jesus did for all of us.

  I don't want you to get the impression from what I've written thus far that Mom and I think we blew our chance to lead you into a relationship with Christ and a commitment to the work of his Kingdom here on earth. Actually both of us did a lot of things of which, upon reflection, we're quite proud. Mom went out of her way to make you into a caring person. Both by word and example, she taught you the kind of religion that the Apostle James so much admired in his epistle.

Pure religion and undefiled before God and the Father is this,
To visit the fatherless and widows in their affliction, and to
keep himself unspotted from the world.

James 1:27

Mom always made it her special mission in life to visit
and give special attention to older ladies whom everyone else
seemed to have forgotten or left behind. Wherever she
traveled, she made sure to send postcards to her special
elderly friends. She visited them faithfully and often took you
along with her. There was Mrs. Henry who served as a house-
keeper for the family next door to us and was also a member
of our church in Philadelphia. Whenever possible, Mom used
to drive her to and from church. Mom also took her to lunch
and gave her little gifts from time to time. Once she spent
Christmas Eve with us.

When Mrs. Henry was hospitalized, Mom may have been
her only regular visitor. She took you along on some of those
visits, and I remember that you and Mom were the ones who
packed up Mrs. Henry's things when she had to move. I'm
sure that something of what it means to be a Christian in ministry to others rubbed off on you as you helped Mom to help
her friend.

Mom also visited Mrs. Rue, a widow who, in the end, had
nobody in the world but your mom to look after her. Her only
relatives were in Texas and too far away to do very much. So
Mom took over and became Mrs. Rue's family. Mrs. Rue was a
chain smoker, and your mom hated smoking, but she loved
Helen Rue. She was an interesting old woman who read a lot
and listened well, so visiting her always made for an interesting time. Mom got you involved with Mrs. Rue, who had
never had any children, and she enjoyed you very much. You
visited her on your own from time to time, and I remember
one Christmas Day when you took dinner to her and visited
while she ate it. Your visits to Mrs. Rue were far more frequent
than one might have expected from a high school or college
kid. Mom's unselfish giving of herself and her ongoing concern for Mrs. Rue were beautiful things for you to see. In the
end, it was Mom who looked after Mrs. Rue during her dying

days in the hospital. That had to have had an impact on you. I don't know of anybody who looks after lonely old ladies like your mother does.

Most of all, Mom must have patterned for you the biblical admonition to honor one's mother and father. She always made sure to be close at hand to respond to her parents whenever they had any needs. As Grandmom and Grandpop grow older, Mom has always been there for them. She is ready to drop everything at a moment's notice if one of them has to be driven to the doctor. She is willing to give up her much-needed vacations, as she did on at least two occasions when one of them happened to be hospitalized. The way she calls, visits, and writes to her parents would be a Christian model for any kid growing up. You had to have been impressed. If someday you look after Mom and me when we're old, I'll have to attribute your good Christian character in these matters to what you learned from your mother.

I did some things, too, that were designed to influence you for Christ. I was constantly trying to figure out how to impact your life in such a way that you would become a solid Christian and make the crucial decisions of your life under the leading of the Holy Spirit. Among the ways Mom and I decided that I might make this happen was for me to take you along as a traveling companion. Since my work required that I travel a lot, we decided that you should go along with me as often as possible. This was not an easy decision to make, because, when you were growing up, we could not easily afford the cost of those extra plane tickets. As Mom and I both look back on your growing up years, however, we always say that the cost of those trips was some of our best spent money. I would strongly recommend what we did to any parent who is torn between the need to be with his or her children, on the one hand, and extensive travel demands, on the other.

Taking you on the road with me allowed us some of the best quality time we ever had together. Because you were in school, most of our trips took us away from home over weekends. On a typical trip, you and I would be together for twenty-four hours a day, for two and a half days. We did a lot of talking and getting to know each other during those times. We talked about lots of things, and I had the chance to share my values and viewpoints on everything from sports to race relations. By the time your sports activities at school put an end to most of those excursions, I am sure that you had picked up a pretty comprehensive image of what I was all about and what I believed about God and the world in which we live.

Once, when the two of us were up in New York, we came upon a demonstration against a porno movie that was being shown at one of those skin-flick theatres just off Times Square. This particular movie, entitled *Snuff*, was undoubtedly one of the most obscene, dehumanizing movies ever made. Its climactic scene was reported to be one in which the prostitute (the main character) is slashed to death by two of her psychotic patrons. In order to create realistic panic in the death scene so as to provide the optimum "pleasure" for the sick kind of male sadists who would pay to see such horror, word had it that the film's producers had had the woman who played the part actually murdered in front of the cameras. The film was advertised as having been made in Brazil, "where life is cheap."

There was a crowd of ardent feminists picketing the show. As they marched in a circle in front of the theatre, I decided that it would be a good thing for us to join with them. They were chanting in opposition to the film, "Life is never cheap! Life is never cheap!" We picked up on their chant and demonstrated with them. To my surprise, one of the women participating in the demonstration began to yell at us. "What are you doing here? You're just like them!" she shouted, indicating the men in line to buy tickets. "All men are sadistic animals that ought to be castrated!" I yelled back, "All men are not the same, and we have a right to be here! You've got no corner on opposition to the brutalization of women!"

After it was over, a couple of hours later, we went to a burger place and had a long talk about what the demonstration meant. I tried to make you understand that what those women were doing in that demonstration was very Christian and that my big regret was that the church was not visibly represented. I pointed out that Christianity is not just about getting people into heaven when they die, but also about creating a just and loving society in this world. I tried to get you to

realize that the kind of just society that Jesus wants us to create in his name is one in which women can enjoy their God-
given dignity. I told you that the church too often ignores what
men do to women, particularly if those women are their wives.
I pointed out to you that being a Christian requires that you
champion the rights of women. In our long discussion I also
had the chance to explain that a lot of men who are psychologically sick get some kind of perverted enjoyment out of
humiliating and hurting women; that this happened often
enough so that some women ended up being suspicious of all
men; and that the woman who had tried to get us to leave the
demonstration was, in all likelihood, one of them. In that discussion I think we got into a lot of stuff that fathers and sons
don't often get into.

Another time we went to Fort Wayne, Indiana, on a trip that
proved to be memorable for what didn't happen. Most of the
weekend we sat in boring meetings and had little of interest to
keep us entertained. You got a pretty good look at the tedious
and dull side of my life. After that, whenever people alluded
to how interesting my job must be, you would jokingly say to
me under your breath, "There's always Fort Wayne," and we
would laugh. It was our secret "in" joke.

I think that every kid should have a clear idea about what his
father does for a living, and there's little doubt that you knew
what was involved in my job long before you were twelve
years old. Whether or not you realized it, your going along
with me on those trips helped *me*. You constantly asked the
"whys" and the "wherefores" about everything I did. You
asked me a lot of questions that I should have been regularly
asking myself but probably would not have had you not been
there. Those questions forced me into a lot of healthy self-exam-
ination and helped me to ask questions about my integrity and
about the validity of what I believed was my Christian calling.

Also, you may have kept me out of trouble. Traveling as I do
to various religious gatherings, I see a lot of preachers and
Christian musicians get themselves into compromising and
morally dangerous situations that they would never have gotten into if they had had one of their kids along. It is a difficult
thing to keep your guard up when you are all alone—which is

probably why the early church sent its evangelists out in pairs. If you have to do extensive traveling in your chosen vocation, I hope that you remember our many trips together. I hope that you deem those times of sufficient importance in molding your character and helping you to become a Christian that you will plan to take your kid along with you. There's nothing you can ever do to make up for time you might have but didn't spend with your kid during those precious formative years.

The thing that I consider to be the most important single effort I made to instill within you a Christian value system was taking you to Haiti and the Dominican Republic. I figured that if you could see for yourself the way that most poor people live in Third World countries, you would understand how privileged you were by comparison. I wanted to explain to you the responsibilities that go with privilege. I longed for you to understand the biblical declaration that "unto whomsoever much is given, of him shall be much required" (Luke 12:48).

The first trip was when you were just twelve years old. I had to go to the Dominican Republic to check on some of the missionary work sponsored by the Evangelical Association for the Promotion of Education, the organization that Mom and I helped to create in order to implement our vision for service to the hurting, hungry people of the world.

I vividly recall watching your reactions as you stood on the roof of one of our clinics, overlooking the river-edge slums of Santo Domingo. You stood there motionless with an almost blank expression on your face as you surveyed the horror of what lay stretched out before you. There were an estimated forty thousand people squeezed into that deplorable squalor, without any fresh water or sanitary facilities. There were kids walking barefoot through slimy paths where excrement mixed with mud. Dirty children, dressed in rags or just plain naked, seemed to be standing in front of every shack. Not even the hot noonday sun could make that dismal scene seem bright.

You stood there taking in the sight for almost five minutes. I think you would have stayed longer if I hadn't tapped your little head and told you that it was time to go. I can't be sure about how that scene affected you, but I sensed that you were shaken in ways that would make a lasting impression.

When you were twenty, I took you with me to Haiti. We were to participate in the dedication of a school and an orphanage that had been constructed with funds that we had raised. I'm sure that whatever horrors you saw in the Dominican Republic must have seemed mild compared to the agonies you witnessed on that trip. You were older then, a "cool" Ivy-League university student, and probably more ready for what you experienced. I wanted you to be there anyway, because I knew that you were near the time when you would be making a decision about your life's work. Perhaps, I thought, if you could once again feel the pulse of a suffering people, you would want to commit yourself to meeting human need.

How could you help but be impressed by what our limited efforts for the Haitian people had accomplished? There, among the dirty, depressed conditions of that Haitian town, were the shining bright smiles of the hundreds of kids who were in our school and orphanage. You must have seen that we had made a difference. There's no reward for hard work and sacrifice that can compare with the joy that comes from sensing you have made life better for some hitherto hopeless children.

Whenever I talk to parents who want to know something they can do to influence their children in such a way as to turn them away from the materialistic values of our society and turn them on to Christian living, I always tell them about our trips to the Dominican Republic and Haiti. I contend that a few weeks in the context of social and economic oppression can utterly change a youngster's world-view and cause the kid to rethink what life is all about. That's why I have my office work so hard at arranging such trips for parents and their kids. I believe that kids from middle-class American homes need that kind of experience.

When you reflect on how Mom and I tried to channel your life, I hope you will think well of us. Undoubtedly, we made mistakes, but we tried hard to do the best we could. In the end, I don't think that parents play the determinative role that they think they do in what their children become. Kids have wills of their own. We parents can provide experiences and training as best we know how, but young people decide for themselves what to do with what parents give them. I think parents take far too much credit when their kids turn out great and far too much blame when their kids mess up their lives. After all, God created two perfect children in Adam and Eve. He placed them in a perfect environment, yet both of them rebelled and did evil. Such can be the consequences of having children with wills of their own. I can only pray that you will continue to will the will of God.

Love,

Dad

*   *   *   *

Dear Dad,

People are often surprised when I tell them that I didn't accept Christ until I was a sophomore in high school, as if being your son should have guaranteed my salvation from birth. They're even more surprised when they discover that it was a kid on my high-school soccer team and not my evangelist father who led me to make that decision.

For some reason, it's difficult for those people to understand that while there're a lot of things that parents can give to their children, a relationship with God isn't one of them—even if one of those parents is a big-time preacher. All of the things you talked about doing for me in your letter were important, but at best they brought me to the place where Christianity was a real possibility. Only God can do the actual work of salvation. Paul says in Ephesians 2:8–9, "For it is by grace you have been saved, through faith—and this not from yourselves, it is the gift of God—not by works, so that no-one can boast. For we are God's workmanship, created in Christ Jesus to do good works, which God prepared in advance for us to do."

As you pointed out, though, some of the things you did made it harder, not easier, for me to take Christianity seriously. In fact, I still think you underestimate the problems your failure to "practice what you preach" have caused for me over the years. I'm glad that you are uncomfortable with yourself in light of the things that you proclaim about Jesus and the simple lifestyle, because I am convinced that your proclamation is right. Beyond being right though, you speak God's truth with passionate intensity. The people who assume that you live in a modest home and deny yourself in order to provide for the needs of others have every right to expect that of you at this point, never mind that you might responsibly choose a safe community or maintain high expenses related to your work. You have taken a stand out there.

No one except God can rightly judge another person's spending, and no one should try. But as your son, I think I can ask you to ask yourself one important question: Relative to no one else's, since every situation is unique, how does your lifestyle reflect the self-denial of Jesus? That clears away all the special circumstances and the problem of deceptive appearances. I'm not asking how much you give, but how much you *give up*—for isn't that the real meaning of Jesus' story of the widow's mite? You don't have to answer to anyone but yourself and God, but until you tell me that you are at peace with your lifestyle, why should I or anyone else let you off the hook of your own demands? And please don't try to convince me that your sacrifice comes in the form of the incredible amount of time you spend preaching and teaching and doing the work of the Kingdom, either. It is in your use of time, even more than in your use of money, that I think you have failed to live up to the things you say.

You used to have a great sermon called "The Protestant Work Ethic and the Spirit of Capitalism" that used Max Weber's classic text as a starting point. I don't remember all the twists and turns, but the basic theme was that somehow Martin Luther and John Calvin had fully convinced Protestants that prosperity and achievement were the marks of salvation, with the result being an incredible obsession with work. This work ethic was the driving force behind the rise of American capitalism to worldwide pre-eminence, you said, but it also created a nation of people who confused what they did with who they were. You explained that Jesus cared more about the heart and soul of people than about what they accomplished in the world. The fruit of the Spirit was not property, but rather "love, joy, peace, patience, kindness, goodness, faithfulness, gentleness, and self-control" (Galatians 5:22–23). "What you are," you concluded, "is far more important than what you do." It was a good sermon, Dad. I wish you had been there to hear it.

Because of all the people I know, you derive your sense of value from what you do more than anyone. How else can you explain the ridiculous schedule you maintain, which keeps you from developing normal friendships or staying healthy or even seeing your darling son as much as you should? To everyone else you preach that to have a close relationship with God is the most important thing in the world, yet you drive yourself as though God would rather have you work for him than be with him. You say you sometimes wonder why you don't take personal retreats more often, but you know the answer already—you are too busy. You are too busy for your support group, too busy for your family, too busy for exercise, too busy to develop friendships with non-Christians, too busy to disciple younger believers, and, by your own admission, too busy to spend a day with God. You're so caught up with doing for God that you have no time to be with him. I know that people are constantly after you to speak more and write more and raise more money for missions and everything else, and those are all good things, but isn't the point of serving God to get to know him in a more intimate way? If by serving him, you are hurting yourself and failing to develop a more Christ-like character, can that really be God's will? Maybe you think I'm way off base in all of this, but at least I want to pose the question: Is your lifestyle really causing you to grow closer to Jesus? And if it isn't, do you really think Jesus has called you to sacrifice your own faith for the sake of everyone else's?

Dad, please don't get me wrong; I don't think you're some sort of stubborn, willful hypocrite. Nobody ever resolves these things perfectly or once and for all—certainly not me. The reason I'm so aware of them in the first place is that I have the same problems myself. I don't live the way you do, of course, but I'm not in the same demand, either. Even so, I struggle with my lifestyle and keep asking myself what Jesus calls for and how I will respond. I'm often consumed with "doing" myself, as if there were some way I could earn God's love by accomplishing great things on his behalf. A friend of mine once asked me this simple question: "If you were locked in an empty room for the rest of your life and could not do anything at all, do you think God would love you as much as he does when you are preaching the Gospel and working with inner-city kids?" My head says yes, of course, but my life says that I'm not so sure. Christian service is supposed to be our grateful response to God's grace, not our attempt to merit it. Sometimes I run so fast telling people about it that I forget to experience that grace for myself. I have picked up a lot of good things from you, Dad, but you and I both are probably going to have to deal with accepting our self-value apart from our accomplishments for as long as we are alive. Value comes from God, and that value is infinite for all people. So, as far as I'm concerned, and I know as far as God is concerned, you are the most wonderful man imaginable even if you never speak or write or achieve anything ever again. You are not what you do. You are what you are, and I love you.

Before you worry too much about how your own shortcomings affected my openness to the faith, though, let me tell you that you were and are the best argument I have ever known for accepting Jesus Christ. What was most remarkable to me as a boy was not that you failed to live up to everything, but that you succeeded in living up to so much. Your relationship with God never seemed to be wrapped up with a set of rules and regulations, but I saw the difference it made in your decisions, and I respected you for trying to make your life into what you sensed God wanted it to be. You were right about the benefits of our trips together and my time visiting shut-ins with Mom, and especially about showing me the realities of Haiti and the Dominican Republic. All of it was important. Yet, as good as all those experiences were for me, I didn't make the connection between the way God worked in your life and the way he wanted to work in mine; I was not even all that sure whether or not I believed in God in the first place. That you and Mom were sincere and kind, I never doubted, but that you were right about God, I did doubt. I dutifully went to church because I didn't want to make a big deal about it, and I enjoyed going places with you because you were fun to watch, but most of the time I don't remember feeling anything at all about God, and in my heart I never considered myself a believer. Besides, I had enough to worry about already as a kid. I didn't need any hassles from on high.

I went through elementary school as a little kid with a big mouth, which meant I got beat up a lot and didn't have many friends. "Don't worry," you said, "when you get to junior high school, there will be soccer and basketball teams, and once you're a star player you'll have more friends than you'll know what to do with." You were correct in your prediction, but to a cynical kid like me, popularity through minor celebrity seemed pretty shallow, and I remained something of a loner even when I became popular.

I didn't let that popularity fool me until I made the varsity soccer team as a high-school sophomore. Suddenly I was running with an older crowd, and I quickly became enamored of all the attention, especially after I became the starting goalkeeper on the team. The other goalie was a senior named Joel Dragelin, and he was expected to beat me out, but I did very well early on, and it became a real battle between the two of us. I was supremely confident, though, and I let Joel know it every chance I got. He was gracious to me, but I tried to psyche him out by treating him badly and showing off in front of the coach. I probably didn't deserve it, but I was the starter when the season opened, and Joel's chance to oust me was ruined when he caught his hand under a lawn mower while trying to remove a stick. The doctors managed to repair his severed middle finger, but there was no way for him to play after that.

If I had been Joel, I feel sure that I would have hated the arrogant punk who had taken my place. I probably would have cheered every time the ball got past him for a goal, if indeed I went to the games at all. Joel, however, was anything but bitter. As a matter of fact, he went out of his way to be nice to me. At the games, he carried my equipment bag and brought towels out to me between halves. When I was beaten by a shot, he stood behind the goal and encouraged me.

"You'll get the next one," he would say, while showing me how to correct my mistakes.

Strangely enough, instead of making himself my enemy, he became my biggest supporter throughout the season. That probably would have impressed me more had I not been so caught up in the excitement of being on a winning team and so thrilled by the acceptance of the other players; in fact, I didn't take much notice of Joel at all until after I had blown the big game at the end of the season. Soccer was over, and I was abandoned like a used pop bottle by the rest of the team.

Only Joel stayed interested in me, stopping me in the hall to say hello or telephoning to ask me to go out and do something with him and his friends. I hesitated at first, but after a while I jumped at his invitations—it wasn't as though I had a lot of options. Besides, Joel impressed me. He was one of the most popular kids at our school, and he had befriended me even though I had treated him badly.

I should have guessed that he was a Christian, but I didn't even think about that until he invited me along to his youth group one night. It was one of those "mega" youth groups, with two hundred kids and a rock-and-roll band, and even though I wasn't very excited by all the God-talk, I liked being there, Joel was a big wheel, and he made sure everyone was nice to me. I decided to go again the next week.

After that, things happened pretty fast. I still didn't believe in God, but Joel did, and he talked to me about it every chance he got. At the same time we were becoming close friends. One Saturday morning he picked me up early, and we went out to breakfast at McDonald's.

"Bart, I can see that you know the basics about Christianity from your folks already, but I don't think you know God yourself at all," he said, after we had finished eating. "You've got head knowledge, but that doesn't matter very much. I guess what I want to know is, have you ever thought about really becoming a Christian?"

I hadn't up until then, Dad, despite everything you had done to try to get me thinking about it. But at that McDonald's I decided that even though I didn't believe in God for sure, I desperately wanted to have the kind of faith and joy that Joel and his friends at that youth group had.

I prayed to accept Christ that day, hoping that somehow, somewhere, I would get the faith to back up my prayer. I wish I could say that it came at that moment, but it didn't. What really happened was that I "faked" my faith for a few months while I waited for something to happen. That's right, Dad, I faked it. I went to youth group, read my Bible, cut out a few big sins, and hung out with Joel a lot, pretending I was experiencing things that I wasn't. I even prayed to a God I wasn't sure of, asking him to make himself real to me the way he was real to Joel and to the other kids and the way he was real to you. Some might say I was lying then, but I think "seeking" is a better word because I was in earnest and, in the end, I received what I was after. Somewhere in the midst of going through the motions, my faith became real.

I know so many people who wish they could believe in God, because they're sure that something is missing from their lives, and I sympathize with them. Without God, the universe becomes a harsh, cold reality without meaning or purpose, and most of us don't have the courage to face up to it without despairing.

Believing in God, however, requires more than just a heartfelt desire. Would-be believers must be willing to come to the place in their lives where faith becomes a genuine possibility. An adulterer without faith doesn't need to repent in order to win God's love, but he probably needs to repent in order to be able to believe in that love. Sometimes faith requires stepping out of willful disobedience. Sometimes it requires setting aside enough time to read and think and pray to the God in whose existence you don't yet believe. Sometimes faith requires the seeker to spend time with believers and to experience the love of God second-hand. There are no universal answers, but going through the motions is only a lie if you are not really hoping to find anything, and it may very well be the first step toward genuine faith: "For everyone who asks receives; he who seeks finds; and to him who knocks, the door will be opened" (Matthew 7:8).

You weren't the one who prayed with me when I made my decision to follow Christ, Dad, but I think you had a lot to do with bringing me to the place where faith was a genuine possibility. All those trips and conversations and demonstrations with you and the visits with Mom were part of the way God worked out my relationship with him.

The assistant coach of our soccer team, Sam Holt, used to make us tuck in our jerseys, polish our cleats, pull up our socks, and anything else that would give us a respectable appearance. "Men!" he would bark like a drill sergeant, "if you *dress* like a soccer team, and if you *act* like a soccer team, and if you *practice* like a soccer team, one of these days when you least expect it, you might actually *play* like a soccer team!"

That same principle applies to a lot of things in life. When I was growing up you walked me through the motions of being a Christian, and you lived like a Christian yourself, and you left it at that. Some of the stuff you did may have confused me, but for the most part, I knew what you were all about, and your life helped make faith a genuine possibility for me. What more could I ask of you, Dad? The rest was up to God. It always is.

Love,

Bart

THREE

THE PAINS OF GROWING UP

Dear Dad,

Fifth grade was a rough year for me. Like a lot of other schools at the time, my school was experimenting with what was known as the "open classroom." Normal classroom structure gave way to an independent study format. Each Monday, a list of assignments appeared on the blackboard which were to be completed by Friday afternoon. We still had periods of instruction, but much of the day was left free so that we could do our work in our own way at our own pace. Or, in my case, so that I could fool around all week and then go crazy on Fridays trying to get it all done. I just was not responsible enough at age eleven to handle all of that mid-1970s openness. To make matters worse, I was on the outside of the most popular group of kids in school and had few prospects for getting in. The only break I got that year was in the friendship of Daniel Keough, the biggest kid in the school. He was no better liked than I was, but he kept me from getting beaten up too often, and for that I was tremendously grateful.

Even though I was rejected by the main group, I always knew what they were doing, and I tried my best to do the same in the hopes that they would change their minds about me. When they began buying Adidas sneakers, I begged Mom for a pair of my own. When it became the style to straddle chairs backwards, I did the same, even though it wasn't all that comfortable. I even strained to overhear their conversations so that I would know the correct slang to use at recess. So it followed that when they began to carry around their People Cards, I did the same.

I don't know if you remember about the People Cards, Dad. In a flash of inspired cruelty, the popular kids that year came up with the ultimate weapon to reinforce their domination over the rest of us. One day I noticed a few kids snickering over the index cards they were passing back and forth. It took me a while, but eventually I discovered that each of those cards was dedicated to one of the kids in our class. They were like some sort of home-made baseball cards. Each card was marked with the kid's name and a crude cartoon drawing of his face. A brief paragraph underneath the caricature described the "pros" and "cons" of that person, which was either glowingly positive or viciously negative, depending on that person's position in the school pecking order. Finally, there was an overall rating on a scale of one to ten.

As I think about it now, I can still remember the fear that those cards inspired in me as each of the popular kids developed his or her own collection. Did they have a card about me, I wondered, and if they did, what did it say? There was no way to find out, of course—People Cards were a private joke—but even though I never saw my card, I immediately knew what it must be like, and it hurt me. Yet, incredible as it seems, what hurt me most was not the hatefulness of those kids but rather the knowledge that I was unacceptable to them.

Rather than seeing their cruelty, I believed them. Instead of being put off, I wanted to fit in all the more. So I began a collection of People Cards myself, thinking that if I showed it to a few of the popular kids and they liked them, I might earn some points and gain their favor. I worked hard on my cards, too, struggling to make them clever enough and mean enough to win me a position among the elite. Strangely enough, that is exactly what happened. My cards were a hit. For a few weeks in the middle of my fifth grade year, I became a full-fledged member of the same group of kids who had, until then, treated me as a complete outsider.

I thought that popularity would be the greatest thing in the world, but when it finally happened to me, I was unsure of what to make of it. I was still insecure, and I was particularly uncomfortable with the way my newfound acceptance affected my friendship with Daniel Keough. It simply wouldn't do for a new insider to have too much contact with a confirmed outsider, and instinctively we both knew that. I drifted away from him, and he let me go without saying very much, which saved me from facing up to my betrayal directly.

Whether I admitted it or not, though, I had a very real sense of uneasiness about my newly won position and my new group of friends as well. For all of their good looks and correct clothes and prestige among the rest of the school, the popular kids weren't all that nice, even to one another. Like it or not, though, I had become one of them, and there was no turning back—until you found my People Cards.

You were waiting for me on a Friday afternoon when I came home from school. As soon as I walked in the door, I knew that something was very wrong. To begin with, Mom was nowhere to be found, neither was Lisa. What made things even more suspicious was the fact that you weren't usually the parent on duty when it came to being home to prepare my after-school snacks. To top it off, you obviously were not happy. Still, you waited until after I had had some juice and cookies before asking me to come into the living room for a talk.

"Bart," you began softly, "I wasn't rooting through your stuff at all, but you left some things on the steps today, and when I was moving them I found these . . ." and you pulled out the cards in their little box, "and I wanted to ask you what they were."

How could I answer you? I had avoided the truth until then, but as soon as I saw those cards in your hands, I knew that I was all wrong. I explained myself half-heartedly. You listened quietly for a while, and even after I had finished you didn't yell at me or tell me what a rotten person I was. You just told me how mean you thought the cards were and that it was wrong to judge people by such shallow standards. You asked me what I thought Jesus would think of such cards, and you told me that you weren't angry, really, but that you were just very disappointed in me. Hearing you say that was worse than a beating. By that time, I was crying uncontrollably, but you went on talking. Then, just before you left me alone with my miserable self, you said the most liberating words a mixed-up fifth grader who suddenly hated himself could have ever heard: "This really isn't like you at all," you said. "That's why this caught me so off-guard . . . because you're a nice person, Bart, or at least I've always been pretty sure that you were. This just isn't the kind of thing a nice person like you would do."

What perfect words they were for me! Somehow they managed to make me feel both horrible and wonderful at the same time, and, most of all, they gave me the hope that all was not lost. My dad still loved me, even though I had let him down. I wasn't doomed to a life of cruelty because, blessed thought, that wasn't like me at all. Sitting alone and ashamed of myself in that living room, I realized something absolutely crucial. My actions may have been lousy, but I was still a nice person in your eyes. Or at least I could be.

As important as that final affirmation was, though, it was just as important that you helped me to understand exactly why the People Cards were such a terrible thing. Deep down I had been uncomfortable with them all along, but as a fifth grader I didn't have the critical capacity to articulate exactly why they were so wrong. I needed some kind of rationale to go along with my instinctive inclinations, and that is exactly what you gave me. Now I had an explanation, both for myself and for anyone else who cared to ask, and that explanation was the weapon in my hand that gave me the courage to take my stand.

Kids are pressured into so many things they know are wrong because they aren't able to give themselves or each other honest and good reasons not to do them. It isn't enough to tell young people to "just say no" or to "just do" anything for that matter. Parents can yell and scream about disobedient kids, but unless they're willing to help those kids understand the "whys" behind the rights and wrongs, all the noise in the world will accomplish nothing except create a lot of tension. In that particular situation, you didn't make me do anything at all, but I was grateful because you gave me all the justification I needed to do what I had secretly wanted to do all along.

When I renounced the entire institution of People Cards the following Monday, I went back to being an outsider at school, but I also got back together with Daniel Keough, who was as loyal and affirming a friend as I've ever had. More importantly, I had had my first significant experience of moral crisis and had been shown the way out. That Friday afternoon conversation was an inspired piece of parenting, Dad, and it left an indelible mark on my life.

Of course, elementary school is only the beginning of the peer pressure cooker for a kid, not the end. It gets even worse in junior high, because suddenly there are so many different peer groups from which to choose. It didn't take me very long to figure out that I couldn't just be a kid anymore—I had to be a jock or a brain or a druggie or a preppie or a criminal or . . . something, or else I would be deemed a nothing by default. My problem was that I really didn't know what any of those stereotypes meant as far as my life was concerned. None of those rapidly emerging peer groups was handing out pamphlets outlining the basic assumptions and underlying values of its lifestyle, and there were no introductory lectures or orientation sessions either.

The only way I could find out what one of those peer groups was like was to get inside of it and do whatever the members were doing, to try the group on and see how it fit. So that is exactly what I did, all the way through junior high school and for the better part of senior high school as well. I experimented with different possibilities. You couldn't have missed what was happening with me then, Dad, because every peer group I tried meant that I took on a new identity altogether.

As my groups of friends changed, so did my clothes, my hair, my speech, my music, my taste in girls, my use of time and money, and sometimes my grades as well. I won't bother to review the whole series of "new-look" Barts because there were so many of them. None of them was really me and yet every one of them affected who I became in the end. In one sense, you really had no reason to take them seriously, which is why I'm glad that you didn't make a big deal out of a lot of superficial issues that had nothing to do with what was really going on in terms of my personality.

In another sense, each one of those peer groups had the potential to alter radically the person I was going to become and what my life was going to be about, and both of us knew it. Even though a lot of times I was only playing the part of a jock or a preppy or a little criminal, there was always the chance that I would lose myself in my character or that I would simply do something that I would have to live with for the rest of my life.

I first saw *Rebel Without a Cause* when I was in high school. My youth pastor, who was wise enough to know that sometimes secular films are the most Christian films of all, showed it at church one Sunday night because he wanted to talk to us about the way everybody needs to belong to something. He knew that a group of teenagers would understand and identify with the confusion and desperation portrayed by James Dean, Natalie Wood, and Sal Mineo, and he wanted us all to see that we weren't the only ones who had ever felt alienated, that we weren't alone in feeling alone.

In the movie, James Dean's parents are so weak-willed that they do anything he wants them to and give him whatever he asks from them. He has money and nice clothes, a new car, and those drop-dead good looks to top it off. What he doesn't have, though, is a clear sense of his own identity, and as the new kid in school, that quickly gets him into trouble.

He gets mixed up with a gang of tough guys whose respect he feels he absolutely must earn, no matter what the cost. The night of his big showdown with the leader of that group, Dean realizes that he's in over his head, and he begs his father to stand up to him, to stop him, to save him from his own decisions. But his father can't do it, and Dean storms out of the house on his way to ruining his own life.

It's a powerful scene, full of pathos and adolescent agony, and it moved me when I first saw it. I couldn't have explained it then, but I perfectly understood the way Dean's character was struggling with the overpowering weight of his own free will because I was doing the same thing myself.

Free will is a difficult concept however you approach it. Theologians assert that it is God's greatest gift to humanity and most significant element of his creation, because without free will it would be impossible for us to love either God or one another. Genuine love, by definition, is the free choice of a free individual. Certainly God could have made himself a collection of talking robots that would forever speak of their love for him, but he wanted something infinitely higher than that. So, instead, he created human beings and gave us the potential to accept or reject his will. Our freedom is what sets us apart from every other living thing as human beings—it is the essence of being made in the image of God. A person has to be free, in order to have the ability to love or to understand being loved.

Although God's gift of free will established the possibility of love, so, too, did it create the possibility of sin—and, with sin, every other evil, including death. Truly free people may decide to live in a way that is contrary to the will of God. That is the theme of the story of Adam and Eve, and that is the cause of the terrible injustice and suffering that dominates our world. It is surely not God's will that we hurt and destroy others or that we ourselves be hurt and destroyed, but we are not bound by God's perfect will, and we can do that which he does not want us to do.

Every evil in this world, as well as in our own lives, is rooted in free decisions against God's will—ours or someone else's. Not only are we fallen because of sin—all Creation is fallen as well. While our sins can surely be forgiven, they still have very real consequences for the sinner and those who have been sinned against. When God forgives a convicted murderer and restores that person to righteousness, it is a miracle indeed, but that doesn't mean the person is automatically freed from prison, and it certainly doesn't bring the victim back from the dead or put an end to the suffering of the grieving family. In some sense, what is done simply cannot be undone, and it is for that reason that we can never take our own decisions lightly just because we are sure of the grace of God.

What we do matters, and our choices make a difference, both in our own lives and in the lives of other people. It is when we understand that truth—when we recognize that the decisions we freely make have real and sometimes enormous consequences—that our freedom threatens to become a gift too burdensome to bear. To be free means to be responsible for our own lives and for the choices that we must make, and such responsibility can be a frightening prospect indeed—especially to a young person. It can crush a kid to consider the realities of his own life. For who has more options than a kid in today's youth-oriented society? Who has more choices and decisions to make than a child of the modern western world? Who has more of that burdensome gift called freedom? No one, Dad, no one at all.

As a kid, though, I learned to know better than to complain to an adult about having too much freedom. Freedom is a burden if you have more than you can handle, but it is the world's most coveted commodity when you don't have enough of it. Adults, more often than not, don't have nearly as much freedom as they would like. I felt as though most of the adults I knew envied my freedom when I was growing up.

In fact, some of the most frustrating experiences of my life were when I came to you with my problems and crises only to find that to you they weren't problems and crises at all, but rather blessings in disguise. "Man, oh, man," you would say, "I only wish I had opportunities like the ones you're talking about." What made it worse was that I knew you really meant what you were saying, that you really did envy my opportunities. Nothing is more alienating than having someone tell you how lucky you are when you feel absolutely miserable about your life.

Looking back, though, I can see why you might have reacted the way you did to my situation. In that respect, I am old now. Even though I am only twenty-six, I can't escape the fact that a lot of my big decisions are behind me. Already I find myself asking whether I've made the right choices and wondering what things would be like if I had made those choices differently. There is something ironic about the way kids are always wishing they were grown-ups while so many adults long, and sometimes even pretend, to be kids all over again. For the kids, it's usually just a case of imagining adulthood as being able to do whatever you want and having a lot more money with which to do it. The adults are not misled in the same way. They know exactly what they are wishing for: the seemingly unlimited freedom of youth. Yet to the kid who has that freedom, it doesn't seem like a blessing at all, but rather a curse in disguise. At least that's how it felt to me.

You see, it wasn't just a matter of choosing a few classes or figuring out what skateboard to buy or who to ask to the freshman dance—I was trying to figure out who and what I was going to become, and I was scared to death that I was going to make a mistake. I would have denied it a thousand times under oath, but the truth is that I had my life in my hands, and I didn't know what to do with it.

I think a lot of kids are as confused as I was, even though they won't admit it, even to themselves. On a lot of levels, freedom is a burden to them because even though they have the world at their feet, they don't know what it's for or how to deal with it. Yet everywhere I look, kids are being given more and more freedom and responsibility at earlier ages than ever before—and it is destroying them.

I met Jill at a Bible camp in Wisconsin where I was the speaker. Like James Dean's parents in *Rebel Without a Cause*, Jill's mother and father had left her on her own almost from the beginning, their alcoholism having consumed any interest they might have had in their daughter's life or in her decisions. A very attractive girl, Jill began to date at the age of twelve because having a boyfriend told her that she mattered to somebody. Older boys, sensing her desperate need for love and acceptance, used her vulnerabilities against her. Time and time again, she allowed herself to be taken advantage of sexually in exchange for a short-lived sense of security. Physical relationships took over her life, so that by the time she talked to me at the age of fifteen she had become utterly addicted to sexual contact. As she put it, sex was the only "love" she had ever known.

The reason she came to me was that after hearing the good news of God's unconditional love, she desperately wanted to become a Christian but felt powerless to stop herself from doing what she knew God forbade. Jill believed in the forgiveness of sins, but she couldn't believe that God could heal her emotional wounds and change her into a different person. I tried to convince her, but she went away despairing.

"It's my own fault," I remember her saying sadly. "Nobody held a gun to my head and made me become what I am. I made my own decisions and now I'm going to have to live with them forever."

Jill was only fifteen years old when I talked with her, but she had already given up hoping for anything really wonderful in her own life. She had been burdened with the full weight of her freedom at the age of twelve, with no help or guidance whatsoever to help her bear it, and it had crushed her spirit.

There's a time to let kids make their own decisions, to be sure, Dad. I didn't want you to run my life, and I hated it when you reined me in too tightly. What I did want, though, was for somebody to help me with those tough decisions by making me ask myself the hard questions about them. When you ridiculed my choices, I stuck to them more than ever, even if I knew they were wrong, because I couldn't bear to be humiliated by admitting my mistakes. But when you took the time to help me see the consequences and ramifications of those choices and showed me how they fit in with the better side of my personality, then I felt as though I just might be able to handle things after all.

In order for freedom to be the blessing that God intended for it to be, it must be more than simply having permission to do whatever you want to do so long as you don't encroach on the freedom of anyone else to do the same. That definition of freedom may work well for lawyers and legislators as they manage the government of a city or a nation, but it is sorely inadequate for any of us as individuals. For even after we have liberated ourselves from the bondage of every external force that threatens our ability to do as we please, we find that our own desires can enslave us in a far more inescapable way than we ever imagined possible. It is more obvious in the case of drug addicts and alcoholics, but all of us have to deal with our appetites for things that can destroy us. None of our hearts are pure. When adults look at kids with envy because they can do anything they want to do with themselves and their lives, they forget that what a person wants to do is not always what will make him joyful or satisfied in the end.

One Saturday night when I was about thirteen years old, you came home from a long day on the road to find me in a deep state of depression. Over dinner, while I silently ate my meal, you and Mom talked about the things you had done since breakfast.

"So Bart . . . what did you do all day?" you finally inquired as Mom began to serve dessert.

"Nothing," I replied in a sullen tone of voice. "I did nothing. I sat around and watched television to tell you the truth. It was a lousy, boring day because there's nothing to do in the whole lousy, boring place."

I wasn't looking at you when I said it, which is probably why I didn't stop before I did, but Lisa was, and she quickly asked to be excused. It was too late, though. You were into your tirade before she could even push back her chair.

"Why you ungrateful little kid!" you exploded. "How dare you say there's nothing to do around here when all your mother and I do is work so you can have a nice time. What I wouldn't give for a free day myself! Bored? You were bored? Stop feeling sorry for yourself! What's the matter with you that you can't think of anything better to do than watch television all day? Why when I was your age . . ."

I'll spare you the rest. As heartfelt as your lecture was, I'm afraid you missed the point. You yelled at me for doing nothing as though it was my first choice, when the real problem was that I was just not creative enough to fill in the vacuum of an empty day. Kids are not born knowing how to have fun any more than they are born knowing how to work. They need to be taught. You may have thought you were doing me a favor by giving me so much free time, but all you really did was leave me feeling like a loser because I didn't know what to do with myself. You should have been glad I didn't do something worse, actually, because as Sören Kierkegaard once said, boredom is really the root of all evil. G. K. Chesterton had the same idea when he wrote, "At the end of the day, when the children tire of their toys, it is then that they turn to torturing the cat."

You see, Dad, boredom is always the end product of the kind of freedom that is nothing more than being allowed to do whatever you want. Even when it leads to evil, it only finds its way back to boredom again. The writer of the Book of Ecclesiastes had that kind of freedom, and yet, after pursuing every kind of desire known to man to the fullest measure, his conclusion was this:

"Meaningless! Meaningless!" says the Teacher. "Utterly meaningless! Everything is meaningless." What does man gain from
all his labor at which he toils under the sun? Generations come
and generations go, but the earth remains forever. The sun rises
and the sun sets, and hurries back to where it rises. The wind
blows to the south and turns to the north; round and round it
goes, ever returning on its course. All streams flow into the sea,
yet the sea is never full. To the place the streams come from,
there they return again. All things are wearisome, more than
one can say. The eye never has enough of seeing, nor the ear its
fill of hearing. What has been will be again, what has been done
will be done again; there is nothing new under the sun.

Ecclesiastes 1:2–9

That man had denied himself nothing that he desired, but after
he had done it all and experienced everything the world had
to offer, he was bored. I see the same phenomenon in so many
of the young people I meet. They can do anything they want to
do, but they're bored, and because they're so bored they turn
to drugs and to sex and to crime and to cars and to music and
to video games and even to getting rich and amassing material possessions like their parents. They look everywhere for
excitement and new experiences, always reaching for a higher
high. Sometimes they follow the group and sometimes they
follow their own desires, but in the end, there's not much difference. They turn to those things to escape the burden of their
freedom, and yet, when everything has been said and done
and they have run every possibility all the way through or
been crushed and destroyed by the consequences of their own
decisions, they come to the awful realization that they are
bored all over again. Life to those kids, as to the writer of
Ecclesiastes, becomes meaningless because chasing after
excitement and fulfillment by doing whatever you please ultimately holds no more promise than trying to catch the wind.

As I said before, in order for freedom to be a blessing instead
of a curse, it must be something more than just having nothing
that you *have* to do. Real freedom is not simply being allowed
to do as you please, but rather being liberated from all
bondage—including the bondage of peer pressure and the

bondage of your own desires—to do what pleases God. Jesus came not only to set the captives free *from* something but also to free them *for* something, and that something was and is to choose to do the will of God.

Freedom was never meant to be a moral vacuum where all decisions are equally valid without any "shoulds" and "should nots" or "musts" and "must nots," for God didn't cease to be when he gave us our free will. Instead, he is the hope and the reality that saves us from the crushing weight of what that free will would otherwise become.

"Come to me, all you who are weary and burdened," Jesus says in Matthew 11:28, "and I will give you rest." The rest Jesus gives is not simply being able to do as we please—it's the call to do his will and to do his work, which he promises will be better for us than anything we could desire ourselves: "For my yoke is easy and my burden is light."

I think you understood that when you liberated me as a boy from those horrible People Cards. I was enslaved to my own desire for acceptance at that point, and to simply have let me do as I pleased would have been the crudest kind of freedom. What I needed was real freedom—the ability to do whatever it was that Jesus wanted me to do—and that's what you gave me. When kids fall prey to peer pressure, they are not the victims of the other kids as much as they are the victims of bondage to their own desires. They need freedom, to be sure, but it must be real freedom—the liberation from anything that keeps them from doing the will of God.

Sometimes that means that kids need help in understanding the consequences or possible consequences of a particular decision, and sometimes that means they need a way of explaining what's right or wrong to themselves or to their friends. Sometimes that means having parents who are willing to play the "heavy" so that their son or daughter can say no to something without losing too much face. That happened a few times for me, and I was glad to be able to say, "My dad won't let me," when the truth was that I wasn't sure about what to do.

Curfews work that way, I think. I remember picking up a girl at her house for a first date and being very intimidated when her father told me I had better have her home by ten o'clock or there would be trouble. Something in his tone of voice let me know that I didn't want to cross this man.

His daughter and I had a nice time that night, but when it got close to 9:30, I told her we had better start for home even though the movie wasn't yet over. "Oh, don't worry about that," she said. "My real curfew isn't until midnight. I just had my father say that in case things didn't go well and I wanted to get away from you early. He's got that tough-guy act down so well, I never have any trouble with pushy boys anymore."

That was one sharp father, I think. He gave his daughter freedom in the best sense of the word, and she appreciated it.

Mom had a different way of helping me figure things out, and that really helped me when I was trying on all of those different identities as a kid. It was quite simple, really, and it grew out of her characteristically unlimited optimism. No matter what I was into at the time, she always managed to see some marvelous way in which I could use it to do good.

When I was a "jock," she talked with great excitement about how I might become the kind of coach who makes a difference in the lives of his players. When I ran with kids who were in trouble, she used to speculate on what was troubling them and how I could use my influence to get them back on track. As a high-school freshman, I became obsessed with juggling for a while, which seemed like a pretty neutral thing to me. Not to Mom, though. "Oh Bart!" she bubbled. "Imagine all the joy you could bring to people in old folks homes and hospitals as a juggler. That would be so exciting!" She even bought me a set of special juggling pins and rings to spur me on.

The genius of her enthusiasm was that it never depended on what I was doing—she found glorious possibilities in everything I tried. Her unspoken message was very clear to me at the time; I was free to become anything I chose to be because no matter what I did, it could and must be done for God and for the good of his people.

That's what real freedom is, I think: the understanding that in a world filled with choices and decisions, under tremendous pressure from other people and our own desires, amid the paralyzing fear of mistakes or failure, loving God and loving his people are the only things that really matter, and doing those things is a decision that we genuinely have the ability to make in every situation.

You and Mom didn't let me do whatever I wanted to, Dad, but you gave me my freedom, nonetheless. I think I finally appreciate it.

Love,

Bart

*   *   *   *

Dear Bart,

Your fifth-grade year was an easy one for me to remember. It was a time when the spontaneity that had always been the hallmark of your personality was eclipsed. You were trying to make that shift from defining yourself from what you thought I thought of you to defining yourself as what you thought the kids at school thought of you. It was a hard time because you knew you were great as long as your identity was provided by me. Growing up, however, required going beyond your dad and finding your identity in the messages that came from those significant others called peers. That year, the messages you were getting from your peers weren't very positive.

You were a kid with a lot of natural athletic ability at a time in life when athletic ability was pretty important, and I think some of the kids in school were jealous of you. You had been to a lot of places and done a lot of things that enabled you to play one-upmanship with them and win. Most importantly, you were extremely verbal. Your vocabulary and ability to express yourself allowed you to dominate conversations without your even realizing it. Consequently, you posed a real threat to a lot of those boys in your fifth-grade class. Shutting you out may have been more the result of their defensiveness than the result of your failure to be "cool" in their eyes. Regardless of the cause, you were hurting.

Another reason that year was tough was that up to that time, you and John Baxter had been such close friends that you were really more like brothers. His parents were good friends of ours, and his dad was a professor at Eastern, too. The campus was the "backyard" for both of you, and you did virtually everything together. Fifth grade was a time when you and John each felt the need to widen your horizons, and that translated into the two of you going your separate ways. Sometimes you even fought. Both John's parents and Mom and I believed that we had to stay out of it and let you boys work things out. It was tough for all of us, but it was the right thing to do. In the end, it was as though you guys really were brothers, because it was John who was the best man at your wedding, but in the fifth grade, splitting up with your best friend was an almost unbearable grief.

Parents who care always find that when their kids hurt, they hurt, too. Mom and I talked long and hard on the question about what to do. Mom even made a secret visit to school to get your teacher's perspective on the problem. She found that the teacher was well aware that you were shut out of the "in" clique of boys in that fifth-grade class. She was very much tuned in to the not-too-subtle cruelties that were played out on a daily basis within her classroom. The suggestion was made that you ignore the "in" clique. There were other kids in your class who could be your friends and who weren't playing the kinds of exclusionary games that those mean kids were playing with their People Cards.

First of all, there was your true-blue friend, Daniel Keough. Daniel was a kind of counterculture kid, who, in the best sense, scoffed at what the "in" kids were all about. Then there was Rocky Walker. Rocky, like you, was outside the "in" group, but he didn't seem to care. He was a good-looking guy and a great athlete. Your teacher thought that Mom and I should engineer your getting together with Rocky so that the pain of being excluded from the clique would be forgotten in a new friendship. We tried to do just that, but we learned that parents can't really determine what friendships do and do not work for their kids. You and Rocky did not become best friends that year, but I guess your teacher wasn't too far wrong in her suggestion because you and Rocky did become friends during high school, and he was a groomsman at your wedding.

Finding those People Cards wasn't difficult. You always seemed to carelessly leave things around in full view of everyone. I believe I found them one evening after you had gone to sleep. They were lying on the steps that went up to your third-floor bedroom. They upset me, but they also gave me a chance to do something that I think has served you well ever since. They gave me the opportunity to show you that the group you would have given almost anything to join was not worth joining; that if you did join the "in" clique, it might be at the expense of being the kind of person Jesus would have you be. Such an opportunity was not to be passed up, and, as you recall those painful events, the confrontation over the People Cards was all that I hoped that it would be. I think the thing that really got you away from trying to be like those mean kids was the realization that being like them required things that would never do for a follower of Jesus Christ.

I do not want to give the impression that I think that all peer groups are bad for growing boys. It is just that parents should be sure that the social roles prescribed by any peer group their sons or daughters seek to join allow for living out a commitment to Jesus. Unless a peer group allows a child to do loving things for others, parents must be ready to do everything in their power to get their kids out of it. Being good parents requires discernment with regard to your child's friends.

From what you wrote to me in your last letter, I guess we did help you in your choices of friends. Mom, particularly, helped you to look at the ways in which the various peer groups you joined held possibilities for creative service to other people.

Testing various peer groups is part of every kid's quest for identity. As you properly surmised, each group provides an identity for a kid to try on for size to see if he or she is comfortable in it. Fortunately, you never tried to be a part of certain peer groups that could have destroyed you. For instance, almost every school these days has a drug-using gang on campus, which turns out the kids who are "burn-outs." Your school was no exception. You just never gravitated to that crowd. For the record, I would have stepped in and interfered with your life dramatically if you had. It is one thing to give a kid the freedom to find himself, but it's something else to let him destroy himself.

There were times when Mom and I didn't like what you were into, but when we saw that the identities you were trying out weren't going to destroy you, we made ourselves sit back and let you do your thing. At times, you concerned us with the groups you chose. At times, your choices pleased us. Sometimes you entertained us. Except for a brief time when you were in college, you never seriously upset us by your choice of friends.

I don't know what I would have done if you had gotten into a group that was into heavy metal rock music. In some respects, that music is a preference, and kids can always shoot back to their parents that when *they* were teenagers, *their* parents didn't like their music either. It may sound like a valid argument, but I don't think it really sticks.

Today's heavy metal rock is more than a simple matter of musical taste. It is a subculture with its own particular view of life. It is producing too many rebellious, ruined lives to be treated with benign neglect. Its glorification of spontaneous sexual gratification, acceptance of drugs, and fascination with the dark side of life make it an unacceptable social force. When I recognize how much of a role heavy metal rock music plays in unifying kids who thrive on destructive anger and rebellion, I tend to vote for declaring war on it.

I am well aware of the fact that all rock music does not serve such anti-Christian purposes. There are some very positive things going on in modern music. Some contemporary rock and many of those who play it and listen to it give ample evidence to support that case. But when kids are shutting themselves up in their rooms to spend hours immersed in music that glorifies things evil, including Satan, I know that parents should step in.

You may recall that your sister, Lisa, got into all kinds of music when she was a teenager. When that happened, I spent hours listening to her music with her, and we had long discussions on the relative merits of those groups she most admired. As it turned out, there wasn't much to censor in what she had chosen, and in the end she did a lot to educate me about the positive side of rock music.

My appreciation for so much of what the Beatles and Bob Dylan recorded is a direct result of a daughter who educated her father. I did what I think parents must do to protect their kids from self-destruction: I learned what was being put into her head by the music she was into and tried to help her develop a sense of discretion as to what was and was not acceptable.

I really liked what you had to say in your letter about freedom. You showed me that we agree on the subject. Both of us know that freedom can be an incredibly heavy burden for kids and, in most cases, they will try to get rid of the burden by allowing themselves to be controlled by their peer groups. In so many cases, kids who scream for freedom from their parents do so only to become enslaved to the groups they run with both in and out of school.

Erik Erikson, the famous expert on child development, explains that every growing youngster goes through various well-defined stages in the process of becoming an adult. He persuasively argues that there are assigned privileges and responsibilities with each of these stages. It is Erikson's contention that, when a kid is forced to accept the privileges and responsibilities for a stage of development that is beyond him or her, that kid will become disoriented and neurotic. I believe he is absolutely right.

I have often watched with dismay as parents have relinquished all control over their children. Such parents are usually either too confused to give any useful direction to their children's lives or too lazy to put in the time that this kind of help requires. They try to fool themselves into believing that they are really helping their kids to be adults, in reality, most of these parents are copping out of the God-given responsibility of training up their children in the way they should go.

When a pre-teen child is given the privileges and responsibilities that should be reserved for the mid-teen years, that freedom will tax him beyond his ability to handle it. When a kid is an adolescent and is given the privileges and responsibilities that go with being an adult, she often will fall apart. I am sure that a great deal of the not-too-latent hostility that I discern among young people these days is related to their anger over getting what they thought they wanted from their parents—unrestrained freedom.

The seventeen-year-old who has been given a new car, expensive clothes, and no limitations as to where he can go and what hours he must keep, can be the angriest of all kids. He is completely free to do what he wants, but he was given this freedom before he learned to discipline himself as to how to use it.

Obviously, parents can err in the other direction. They can keep their children so restrained that they never have the chance to test their wings. Bart, both you and I can name kids who have been stifled by parents who made too many decisions for them and were overprotective. Parents have to learn how to give the freedom that allows for experimentation with life and, at the same time, keep vigil lest their children burn themselves out.

My own mother was quite adept at maintaining that balance with me. If I demonstrated any sense of equilibrium in dealing with this particular challenge of parenthood, I probably learned it from her. When I was eight years old, my mom would pay an older girl who lived up the street from us to walk me to school. Crossing Philadelphia streets was dangerous, and my school was several blocks away, so my mother paid the handsome sum of a quarter a week to make sure I got there safely.

From the beginning of this arrangement, I despaired of the vast outlay of money for something that I was convinced was totally unnecessary. After much nagging and begging, my mother finally gave in to my request. She stopped paying my escort and agreed to give me the twenty-five cents each week on the condition that I never run to school and that I look both ways before crossing streets.

Years later, when I was bragging about this example of my early independence at a family gathering, my mom told me the rest of the story. Sure, she got rid of the girl who walked me to school, and she let me set out each morning convinced that I was on my own. I was allowed to assume responsibility and to feel free.

What I didn't know was that each morning my mom had followed me to school herself, making sure to stay out of sight. After school, she was always there to follow me home. There were strange people who might mess up a little kid in the city, and she knew it. There were wrong turns an eight-year-old child could take. She wanted me to be free, but she also wanted to keep a watchful eye on me. She figured out a way to do both, even though it took a lot of her time.

When your turn to be a parent comes, Bart, I hope that you, too, learn how to walk that thin line separating the giving of too much freedom from the exercising of too much restraint. That is one of the most important lessons you will ever have to learn.

Allow me to suggest that when your time comes to figure all of this out, you invite the church to help. Get your church to form a Sunday school class or special group for young couples with children so that you, along with other parents, can study together the Christian way to handle your children's need for freedom. It is much too difficult to figure out alone. When parenting becomes difficult, we need the prayers as well as the wisdom and experience of other Christian parents. That's what bearing one another's burdens (Galatians 6:2) is all about.

Love,

Dad

FOUR

GOING BEYOND THE BIRDS AND THE BEES

Dear Bart,

Every father is supposed to talk to his son about sex. I didn't. That expected discussion about the birds and the bees never occurred between us. This was due in part to neglect and in part to design. Undoubtedly, there were some misunderstandings and confusions that could have been avoided had I taught you what I was supposed to teach you about sex. I did, however, try my very best to give you an adequate education about love. I thought that understanding love was far more important than learning about the "plumbing" of reproduction.

When I was in graduate school studying the sociology of the family, my professors often made the point that good sexual relationships usually came from good interpersonal relationships. I remember one of my favorite teachers, James H. S. Bossard, regularly poking fun at those in the field of family studies to whom he referred as being in the "pure orgasm school of thought." His sarcasm was aimed at those in the field who overemphasized the importance of being well informed about sex as a prerequisite to successful marriages and healthy psychological adjustment.

Bossard argued convincingly that ours is a society in which people have become experts on how to relate physically but are sadly inept at relating to each other as persons. He went on to contend that if a man and a woman develop a deep love and respect for one another, then all else will follow. It was his belief that if a man and woman develop a profound friendship

74

(that's right—I said "friendship"), a sexual adjustment is likely to follow.

Conversely, Bossard was convinced that sexual problems that occur between husbands and wives are much more likely to be the result of things that have gone wrong with their friendship than because of anything wrong with them physically or any lack of knowledge of the best techniques of foreplay or positioning.

Maybe it was a cop-out, but part of my failure to talk to you about the physical side of sex was a consequence of my not viewing that side of the sexual relationship as anywhere near as important as the emotional and spiritual dimensions of what goes on between a man and a woman.

I did all that I could to let you know that being married was the most fulfilling experience that a person could have. Mom was and is my best friend, and I did my best to make you ever conscious of that reality. Of course, being friends with your mother has always been a very easy thing.

Mom is a great conversationalist. There are those who may not think of that as a crucial trait for being sexy—but to me it is. To be married to a person who has the capacity to make life interesting makes sex incredibly exciting. People who bore each other out of bed quickly prove boring in bed as well. What people talk about when they are together in the dark is really very important to maintaining a sexually fulfilling relationship. Physical attraction is important, but if there is nothing else, even a gorgeous partner soon becomes tiring to be around.

I think you got a good lesson on how unsexy the physical side alone can be the summer you turned fourteen. Remember, you went with me to Vancouver, Canada, when I taught summer school at Regent College on the campus of the University of British Columbia? I'll never forget that day when we accidentally discovered the nude beach behind the dormitory where we were staying.

It was a hot August day, and we asked some of the guys who lived on our floor where there was a good place to swim and cool off. "Sure," they told us, "just run down the hill behind the dorm and on the other side of those trees you'll come out on a great beach." We didn't ask any other questions, because we never suspected what would follow. You and I got into our bathing suits, ran down the hill, and burst out onto a beach littered with reclining, naked couples. Utterly embarrassed, not knowing what to do, our immediate reaction was to run out into the ocean so as to conceal from everyone else on the beach that we were wearing bathing suits.

As soon as we could, we made our way back to the safety of the dormitory, laughing wildly, but also shocked. As soon as we settled down you said, "That was ugly. Those naked ladies didn't look like I thought they would." On that hot August afternoon, you made an important discovery: Most people don't look very glamorous without their clothes. I hasten to add that things only get worse with age!

At fifty-three, I hope I'm still sexually interesting to your mom. She certainly is to me. Excitement, however, comes more from what we say to each other than from anything else. Sociologists and psychologists have long theorized about the importance of talk in lovemaking, but all of their intuitive knowledge gained empirical validation with the famous Kinsey Report. That study, still the most comprehensive investigation of sexual behavior ever made, gave data gleaned from hundreds of personal interviews and actual tests verifying that women become more sexually excited by talk than by anything they see or touch. As a guy who is getting old, I find that comforting. As a guy in his mid-twenties, you should find that incredibly important.

Tenderness expressed in talk is one of the most underrated aphrodisiacs ever to exist. Thoughtful attention to the other person may be the best form of foreplay, but never wait to be in bed before you evidence that quality. What goes on in the hours before you go to bed is what is most crucial to a gratifying sexual relationship. I experience my most difficult times with Mom when I behave like a selfish clod all evening and then try to get amorous at bedtime. It takes more than a sexual encounter to truly make love. I think a good Bible verse for any married couple who want guidance on how to keep their sex lives alive and fulfilling is Ephesians 4:32:

And be ye kind one to another, tenderhearted, forgiving one another, even as God for Christ's sake hath forgiven you.

Humor is another trait that is essential for maintaining the joy of sex. One of the more memorable nights I ever had with Mom was spent in the remote little town of Geraldine in New Zealand. The two of us were on vacation, and we were looking for a motel for the night. We found one in Geraldine that had a room with a waterbed. We had always joked about trying one of those things someday, and we decided that the day had come.

When we got into bed, everything became wildly funny. Maybe it was the bed or maybe it was us, but neither of us seemed to be able to move without getting the other to bounce up and down as if we were on a trampoline. Once, when I tried to get out of bed, I fell back into the mattress and literally bounced Mom out. We spent hours laughing. We laughed at the bed, we laughed at each other, we laughed at the whole absurd situation—and we felt very close to each other.

Personally, I think that people without a good sense of humor must have a hard time surviving in marriage—or in anything else, for that matter. I consciously tried to let you and your sister know how Mom and I related to each other—that we got along great, cared for each other, had an awful lot of fun together, and that each of us thought the other to be a very special person. Some might ask what all of those things have to do with sex education. In reality, without them, sex becomes little more than a bodily function to relieve tension.

There is something about all of this that does concern me. Did Mom and I paint an unrealistic image of marriage? Did we make it seem too easy? Did we leave you with the idea that we never got disgusted with each other—even to the point of wishing we could chuck the whole thing?

Mom and I did our best not to argue in front of you. I'm sure that from time to time you noted irritation and gruffness between us (usually on my part and seldom on hers), but we never let you in on the really serious conflicts. We had the same problems that most couples have, and sometimes those problems became great crises. Mom and I would both tell you now that, if we had not been Christians, we might have ended our marriage at several points along the way.

Religion used to do that for people. It would keep them together when their marriage seemed to be falling apart. It certainly did that for us. I'm sure that there were times for Mom, and there were certainly times for me, when I felt that marriage was a trap. I thank God that, because of our religious moorings, neither of us viewed divorce as an option for getting out of that "trap." Instead, we always believed that the only alternative was to put things together again and make our marriage work. When love seemed to have died, as it did at times, we did not consider walking away from our marriage. Instead, we worked hard to create love and happiness again—and it always worked.

By doing for each other what lovers are supposed to do for each other, even when we didn't feel like it, we eventually experienced the resurrection of what had been killed; what came to life again always seemed richer and deeper than what we had had before. When people don't allow their suffering to kill their love, working through it together is bound to make their love better. It's been thirty years for Mom and me, and in all honesty, I love her more now than ever before.

I feel sorry for you and your generation, because in today's world not even religion seems to hold people together. Let it be known that as far as I'm concerned, *true Christianity* still provides the glue that can hold people together in a world that's falling apart.

I don't think you were ever really aware of the hard times Mom and I had, because we thought it would be bad for you to know. A kid faced with the kind of pain and divisiveness that are hallmarks of a marriage in trouble is in great danger of being emotionally and psychologically destroyed. I often wonder what happens inside children who have to witness the knock-down, drag-out confrontations that all too often go on between parents in conflict.

In times of extreme frustration, husbands and wives sometimes say things that are horrible and make threats about leaving that can devastate a kid. Such painful exchanges should never take place, but when they do, there is no excuse for letting the children be party to them. It may be that in a day or two the trouble will pass, and the couple may begin to put their world together again, but the kids who have had to watch and hear their parents' worst times, may never get over it. They may harbor secret fears that will haunt them for years and cloud the way they look at life.

Mom and I had some tough times, but we hid them from you for these reasons. At least I hope we did. Not only did we refuse to argue in front of you; we tried to keep you from knowing we had problems at all. Was that a mistake? Did we leave you with the false impression that people simply get married and live happily ever after? Did we keep you from one of "the facts of life" that is far more important than what is usually written up in books with that title?

Another part of what I considered to be sex education was helping you to come to grips with what it really means to be a man in the deepest Christian sense of the word. In many respects, my understanding of manhood was going through a disturbing re-evaluation as you were coming of age. Consequently, I hadn't gotten enough of my act together on this matter to do the kind of job I wished I had done in raising you to be a godly husband. My earlier conception of what it meant to be a man was, for the most part, blown away by the feminist movement. The funny thing is that the feminist movement, which fostered my radical re-evaluation of my role as a Christian husband and father, is condemned by many Christians as being dangerous to the family. I think that what the feminists taught me has brought me a lot closer to what God wills for me to be as a man than did much of what I got from the pulpit while I was growing up.

The feminists taught me that raising children wasn't ordained to be the woman's job. Raising kids is something that should be mutually shared by parents. Unfortunately, I did not grasp this truth until it was a little too late. When you were a baby, I seldom changed a diaper or, for that matter, even babysat in order to give your mom some time off.

Somehow, I'd grown up believing that such things were a mother's responsibility. If I ever did baby-sit for you, Mom was surprised, filled with gratitude, and treated me as though

I'd gone out of my way to do what was supposed to be her job. The idea that the kids were hers and that my job was to be the breadwinner seemed to me to be legitimized by the church.

Preachers and teachers throughout Christendom erroneously allowed many of us to think that this was the way God wanted it. Needless to say, many of us males foolishly encouraged and supported this idea. In Paul's letter to the Ephesians, he writes:

> Submitting yourselves one to another in the fear of God. Wives, submit yourselves unto your own husbands, as unto the Lord. For the husband is the head of the wife, even as Christ is the head of the church: and he is the savior of the body. Therefore as the church is subject unto Christ, so let the wives be to their own husbands in every thing.
>
> *Ephesians 5:21–24*

We took this passage and used it to imply that men had a right to make their wives into people who served them and took care of all the dirty work of keeping house and raising children. Note that we usually didn't go on to fully consider verse 25:

> Husbands, love your wives, even as Christ also loved the church, and gave himself for it . . . .

As I look back on those years when you were a baby, I not only regret what my faulty religion did to Mom, but also how it cheated me. I really missed some of the great joys of life. When I see modern fathers carrying babies, changing diapers, and doing all the other things that go with parenting, I realize that I passed up something very precious. Because I thought it was my right as a man to be free from the responsibilities that go with child rearing, I failed to take advantage of some of the greatest privileges of fatherhood. I hope you have learned enough to be a different kind of husband and father than I was during your early years.

By the time you were about six years old, my views about marriage and child rearing were being challenged by some of the graduate assistants who worked with me at the University of Pennsylvania. They were well read in the feminist literature that was emerging in those days and most anxious to expose the male chauvinism of their would-be mentor. They challenged the idea that a male should be a "macho man" and began to help me to see that a healthy male was assertive but also tender, strong but also sensitive, a leader but also a servant.

The more they talked about what they thought should be male characteristics, the more I realized that they were describing the traits of Jesus. Jesus was a man who wasn't afraid to let people see him cry when he saw loved ones in pain. Jesus was not so into the "male" affairs of life that he was unable to consider the loveliness of the lilies or to feel tender about little children and sparrows. Being the "Lion of Judah" did not keep him from comparing himself to a mother hen:

> O Jerusalem, Jerusalem, which killest the prophets, and stonest them that are sent unto thee; how often would I have gathered thy children together, as a hen doth gather her brood under wings, and ye would not!
>
> *Luke 13:34*

The more my feminist students taught me about being a man, the more I saw in Jesus qualities I had never noticed before. The more I learned of these qualities, the more I wanted you to have them, too. A full understanding of Jesus reveals what being a whole person is all about.

Somehow you got the message of Christ-like manhood in spite of me. There was a precious softness about you that made you into a very special child. When you were in kindergarten, the mother of one of your classmates called to invite you to her daughter's birthday party. She told Mom that you were the only boy invited, but that her little girl wanted you to come more than she wanted anybody else. Mom was curious, did some investigating, and was told by your teacher that this little girl was picked on constantly by the other children in the class. Children can be cruel to one another, and evidently this little girl had become the brunt of everyone's meanness. Everyone, that is, but you. You had become her defender, and the more the other kids picked on her, the more you became

her friend. You just couldn't stand to see anybody sad or suffering. You had the kind of sensitivity that might not be considered "macho" but is certainly in character with Jesus.

Being rough and tumble was never a big thing with you
even though you had the physique to be so. Despite the fact
that you were an all-star goalie and a varsity basketball player,
you were never the kind of guy who wanted to be distin-
guished by toughness. The kind of strength that it takes to be
a pacifist was what I found in you. Even when it seemed to
others that it would have been right for you to haul off and
land a punch or two, you never did.

I remember when you were in the second grade, there was
a boy who rode on your school bus who got some perverse
delight out of humiliating you by spitting on you. You would
come home each day in tears, finding it difficult to handle the
way he embarrassed you in front of all your friends. I pointed
out that you were much bigger than he was and could easily
beat him up. You simply told me that you knew that you
could, but didn't want to. When there was no let-up in the spitting, I ordered you to hit that mean little boy. The spitting
stopped, not because you fought back, but rather because you
told him, "Bill, if you don't stop, I'm going to have to hit you.
I don't want to hit you, but my father told me I have to hit you
if you don't stop. I'm really sorry, but I have to do what my
father tells me."

Little Bill never messed around with you after that. Once
again you had demonstrated what being a Christian man is all
about. You got no joy from being tough even though you were
strong enough to be tough. You had discovered the strength it
takes to avoid using violence. Jesus must have been proud of
you—and he must have been disturbed by my "fatherly"
advice.

I knew that you had broken out of the stereotypical role prescribed for high-school boys when you joined the high-school
chorus. You had already established yourself as one of the
most prominent jocks in the high school when Mom asked you
if you would join the chorus. She had loved going to the concerts when your sister was in high school and had been hoping that you would carry on the tradition. You never even

blinked. Never mind that the macho men on campus probably thought it a bit uncool. Never mind that none of your close • buddies were in the chorus. If that's what your mom wanted, no more needed to be said.

There was one time that the chorus had a concert scheduled the same night as a basketball game. When you asked how that could happen and what other choir members did in such situations, you were told that your high school had never had a basketball player in the choir before. The night of the concert, you sang with the choir. Mom was there, of course, and then she drove you over to the gym in time to join the game that had already started. I thought that was really neat.

Sex education in our home also involved coming down hard on pornography, even though many people expected "real boys" to be into dirty pictures. Back in the 1960s, I had joined the rest of the liberal establishment in contending that pornography was merely an unpleasant sideshow that accompanied freedom of speech. At that time, I found pornography distasteful, but I didn't see it as a threat to your well-being or as an instrument for generating perversion. Fortunately, my ideas about pornography changed before you reached puberty, so that you grew up in a home that was strongly against it. In light of my most recent reflections on the matter, I would be even more outspoken against it than I was when you were growing up.

Today, there is mounting evidence that pornography is addictive. It's not just a naughty thing; according to many authorities, it tends to get a real hold on some people. For reasons that are hard to explain, the addiction is primarily a male problem. The consequences of the addiction, however, should be frightening to both men and women.

Those who become addicted start with the "soft" porn of something like *Playboy* centerfolds. Such photos prove titillating for a while, but they gradually lose their capacity to generate the desired sexual stimulation. Harder forms are then sought and found, but the addict soon finds that even these become inadequate to meet his increasingly perverse hungers. Lust, unlike love, thrives on domination and is fed when the object of lust is helpless and innocent.

People who pride themselves on being open-minded are
• likely to scoff when radio and television preachers suggest that
what begins with *Playboy* may be the first link of a chain that
eventually binds men to finding their delight in sadistic child
porn. In our home, we even took out forms of pornography
that church people all too often accept. We especially down-
graded things like beauty pageants. I have always been a bit
perplexed that the feminist movement has been more opposed
to the Miss America contests than has the church.

Feminists rightly contend that such beauty contests make
women into sexual objects instead of treating them as persons.
It cuts no ice with them when the promoters of those pageants
argue that the bathing suit competitions are only a "small"
part of the contests. The feminists ask why the bathing suit
competitions are included at all. In some beauty contests, the
measurement of the contestants' hips and bust are announced.
The obscenity of that is all too obvious. We would never put
up with any contest that advertised the measurements of the
private parts of men's bodies. So the feminists rightly ask why
we don't protest when the private parts of women's bodies are
measured and made public knowledge.

In our home, we condemned those beauty contests as sexist
institutions and talked about them as exercises in the denigra-
tion of women. We rejected them, along with *Playboy*,
Penthouse, and all the rest because they portray women as sexual objects that exist only to satisfy men. The Campolo view is
that women must always be viewed as persons to be loved and
never as things to be used. If sex education involves helping
adolescents understand the perversity of pornography, I think
you might give me passing grades in this area of your training.

In the same way, I provided an ample critique of dating, making you aware of the inherent evils of the system. To begin with,
I let you know that the facts demonstrate that most teenagers
are incapable of handling the sexually pressurized situations
that go along with modern dating. Both Mom and I tried to help
you see how much psychological strain and hurt is involved in
this "game," which most parents seem to view as innocent fun.

Most guys at fourteen and fifteen are not equipped verbally
to keep a date going for an entire evening and usually lack the

creativity to think of interesting things to do or places to go. Consequently, necking often becomes an escape from the awkwardness of not knowing what to do. Necking allows teenagers to seem sophisticated to each other even in the midst of social ineptness.

With Christian kids, the problems are even more severe because their heavy necking—in which hands go all over the place—leaves them in deep states of guilt. There are always those neo-Freudian psychologists who claim that guilt is a sick reaction to innocent sexual play generated by an overly restrictive church. Maybe there is some justification for this position, but it seldom occurs to these all-too-arrogant critics of religious restrictiveness that the guilt may be a healthy reaction to the violation of the will of God.

I don't know how involved you got in necking and petting, but I have my suspicions. The fact that you found it so difficult to "break off" with some of the girls with whom you went steady, long after you realized that the relationship was going nowhere, used to have me wondering. Guilt can keep a teenager, particularly a Christian teenager, tied into a relationship long after it should have cooled. Somehow teenagers think that if it all happens with people they really love and intend to marry, it will all be OK in the eyes of God. Down deep inside, however, they know better.

Usually, kids who start getting sexually involved turn off to God and the church. Finding it impossible to continue what they're doing and, at the same time, remain close to God, they give up on being close to God. Teenagers often distance themselves from God simply because it's easier for them to do their sexual things that way. I'm not sure how this all worked itself out in your life, but I hope you didn't do yourself or others any harm along the way. In the midst of those turbulent years, I tried to make you ever aware that nothing could separate you from the love of God (Romans 8). I wish that all teenagers who have crossed the lines required for clean sexual relationships would realize that God is still with them and is ready to make them like new again. They should all know 1 John 1:9:

> If we confess our sins, he is faithful and just to forgive us our sins, and to cleanse us from all unrighteousness.

Bart, there were other things about dating that I tried to teach you. I tried to make you aware that in the modern American dating system too many teenagers get left out, and those who get left out are often emotionally crushed. More than half of American teenagers graduate from high school without ever having had a date. The thing that is really rotten about this is that in our society kids often feel worthless if they are dateless. Their own parents usually pity them, and their self-concepts are often reduced to zero. I'm sure that our dating system has much to do with the prevalence of depression among contemporary teenagers.

I think you caught that message because during your high school days most of your going out was with "the gang" that included both guys and girls. Group dating is one of the healthiest things that teenagers can do, and I have a hard time figuring out why church youth leaders don't do more to encourage it.

Group dating is inclusive, and it gives shy kids a chance to have a good time in non-pressurized situations. Teenagers don't have to worry about whether they will have anything to talk about on group dates because when a gang of kids is together the only problem is to find enough time for all of those who want to talk. Group dating also makes it easy to avoid those situations that can lead to morally compromising sexual behavior.

In today's world, teenagers can never be totally free from the one-on-one kind of dating that has become normative. What was amusing to me was your own awareness of what was wrong with the dating system. It seemed as if many of the one-on-one dates you had were basically an effort on your part to make sure that some really neat girls weren't left dateless on important occasions. The fact that you went to at least three senior proms but didn't go to your own is a case in point. You were well aware of the fact that some of your female friends might be left dateless for this ritual of American high school life, and you were always ready to volunteer to get one of them safely through such a rite of passage. I'm sure you had become aware of the absurdity of what the American dating system does to teenagers simply by recognizing how many personable girls were without dates each year as the night of the prom approached.

When all is said and done, it must still be said that I never really sat you down and gave you specifics about the physiological aspects of sex. I depended on the school to do the job, and that was wrong. Too many parents are like I was and feel that the sex education programs of the public school system will do what they know is really their responsibility.

What is taught at school is okay, I suppose, but, because of the laws requiring separation of church and state, sex education must be given in a "value-free" manner. Of course, that's what's wrong with sex education in the public school system.

God has ordained for the sexual act to be laden with spiritual significance, and to treat it as though it were only a physical act is a great distortion. My gripe is not with the school system, which I think is doing what it must do in our pluralistic society. My gripe is with myself.

I should have explained the biblical significance of sex. I should have helped you to see that if two people come together, not just for sexual pleasure, but to express the kind of love that God wills for a husband and a wife to have between them, then the sexual act can be a sacrament that binds two people together to share a creative life.

> And Adam said, This is now bone of my bones, and flesh of my flesh: she shall be called Woman, because she was taken out of Man. Therefore shall a man leave his father and mother, and shall cleave unto his wife: and they shall be one flesh.
>
> *Genesis 2:23–24*

I should have made clear to you all the biblically prescribed responsibilities that go with the sexual act when it occurs within the confines of marriage.

Like a lot of other Christian parents, I left it up to the secular school system to carry out what was my God-given responsibility as a Christian parent. I wish I had it to do over again. Looking back on your developing years, I realize you must have had a lot of sexual struggles in which I was no help at all. I'm sorry.

Love,

Dad

＊　　＊　　＊　　＊

Dear Dad,

When I read the first few sentences of your letter about sex, I began to load up a heavy dose of guilt to lay on you. It always bothered me that you never talked to me about sex straight out, and I figured this was my chance to let you know how I felt. As I read what you wrote, though, I began to realize that you had indeed taught me a great deal about sex and countless related subjects, even though we never had the "big talk." Still, Dad, I think you ought to know just how ignorant I was about the basics of human sexuality as a result of your approach to the entire subject.

Do you remember the old *I Dream of Jeannie* television show, which starred Barbara Eden and Larry Hagman? It was very popular back in the late sixties, and I watched it every week. Television historians are well aware of *I Dream of Jeannie* because of the great controversy it created when it first came on the air.

The problem was that Barbara Eden's genie costume had a bare midriff that showed her navel, and up to that point, a belly button had never been shown on prime-time television. By today's standards, her outfit was positively modest, but the censors of that era refused to permit the show to broadcast until it was altered to cover up her navel.

The whole affair became quite a sensation, and as I read about it in the newspaper as a boy, I remember wondering what the big deal was. It all seemed so silly to me until . . . in a moment of revelation, I grasped the hitherto unthinkable secret of human sexuality: a woman's belly button! So that's where the action is, I thought to myself . . . from that moment until I was thirteen years old! Never mind that everybody had one, that even I had one, I was secure in my understanding. That's right, Dad, until I was a teenager, I thought the belly button was where babies came from—and it was all your fault.

Fortunately for me, you were a social scientist and had an extensive library of textbooks. One time when I was exploring the wonders of your office, I happened upon the then-notorious *Everything You Always Wanted to Know About Sex But Were Afraid to Ask*. As soon as I saw it, I knew it was the book for me, so I smuggled it up to my room and read it cover to cover in one sitting. What a great book that was for a curious teenager, filled with straightforward definitions and matter-of-fact descriptions of everything I could possibly think of—and a lot of things that I hadn't even considered—without either pornographic exaggeration or moralistic value judgments to confuse things. All things considered, it was probably as good an introduction to human sexuality as I could have received. It neither embarrassed me nor turned me on, and it answered my questions without a lot of commotion.

As you pointed out so well in your letter, however, there is a whole lot more involved with understanding our sexuality than simply knowing the physical mechanics of the sexual act, and I relied on you and Mom for most of the rest. I know you think the two of you did a good job, Dad, and I tend to agree with you. The biggest lie the culture tells a kid about sex is that it can be meaningful as an end in itself, that even in the absence of love, two consenting people can use one another for a lot of harmless fun. I may not have understood how it all worked for a long time, but there was never any doubt in my mind that everything from holding hands to sexual intercourse only makes sense when it reflects the emotions and the commitments of a monogamous relationship. I learned that the amount of physical expression should depend on the level of emotional and practical commitment that stands behind it—and on the commandments of God.

Perhaps that doesn't seem like such an earth-shattering truth, but most kids don't learn about it until after they have gone too far. "How far should I go?" is never a question that should be answered in the heat of passion. At that point, it's usually too late to make a good decision. Kids need to be encouraged to think about standards and personal limits for physical relationships before a relationship even starts.

Your insistence that physical expression and commitment need to match up didn't keep me from making mistakes, but it did give me a starting point for setting my standards. It also helped me see that the deepest physical expression should be reserved for the deepest commitment—that sex was only for married people. You got me thinking about sex in terms of relationships instead of in terms of self-gratification, and that made it easier for me to understand how feminism, machismo, pornography, dating, and even marriage either fit or didn't fit together into a Christian point of view.

There is one area of sexuality where your silence really did hurt me, I'm afraid: masturbation. You never told me anything about masturbation—whether it was right, whether it was wrong, or even whether it was a normal thing for me to be concerned or confused about. I was completely unprepared for the flood of mixed emotions that hit me at puberty, but there's no question that masturbation was the thing that caught me most off-guard and the thing that caused me the most unhappiness and self-doubt.

It was also the thing that made me feel the most alone. I didn't know that I wasn't the only person in the world who masturbated or that by the time they're eighteen nearly everyone has had the experience of manipulating their own sexual organs to provide a pleasant sensation. The numbers vary from study to study, but nearly everyone agrees that close to three-quarters of all girls have masturbated and that, as it is sometimes said, 90 percent of boys have had the experience and the rest are liars. The problem is that even though masturbation is very common, hardly anyone talks about it in an open manner. The mere mention of the word "masturbation" is enough to make most people uncomfortable, which may be why you never discussed it with me. Whether it gets talked about or not, though, masturbation is a big problem for a lot of young people (and probably a lot of older people, too).

The problem, of course, is whether or not masturbation is wrong. From the moment I first discovered it—quite by accident, I might add—I always assumed that it must be wrong. It wasn't that I thought all sexuality was sinful. I know better than that. But you had taught me that all sexual activity is intended for relationships, that even holding hands or a goodnight kiss demands some degree of emotional and practical commitment.

Masturbation is something a person does alone, usually secretly, privately. Like most kids, I was always terribly afraid of being caught or found out (why do you think I was so insistent that you never enter my room without my permission?), and that panicky feeling told me I must be doing something wrong. If it was okay, I reasoned, why was I so ashamed?

Moreover, I felt guilty about the thoughts that ran through my mind when I masturbated, especially after I became a Christian. Surely, nobody who truly loved God would think about things like that, I told myself, especially after reading all of the things the Bible has to say about sexual purity.

Then I heard a youth pastor's offhand comment about masturbation being an "abomination before God," and for a while the issue was settled, at least in my mind. My body, however, had some ideas of its own. Despite all of the confusion, guilt, fear, shame, and even the sense that I was letting God down, I felt helpless to control myself for very long. Sometimes I would hold out for a day or two and sometimes for a week at a time, but even though I believed masturbation was wrong, I couldn't stop myself from doing it. Most of the time I even had some of those forbidden *Playboy* magazines hidden in my room.

A pattern emerged in my life—masturbation, guilt, recommitment to abstinence, temptation, failure—that began to have a frightening effect on my self-image. I began to hate myself in a very real way. I felt that I was evil somehow, in the depths of my heart, and that I didn't deserve the grace of God but rather his punishment instead.

Finally, after reading the passage about it being better to cut off one part of your body than for your whole body to be thrown into hell, I resolved to cut into the back of my wrist with a penknife every time I failed, until I either stopped masturbating or lost my hand. That was a terrible time for me.

I wasn't suicidal, but I definitely wanted to hurt myself, and I did. The physical scars I had from that episode are gone now, but I well remember the frustration and the turmoil that brought me to a point of self-mutilation. I see those same feelings in too many kids today, for the same reasons, and it worries me. Somehow we need to bring this issue out in the open and remove the isolation it causes. There are too many people suffering in silence without any help or guidance when it comes to masturbation.

For me, the experience of cutting my wrist was a turning point. I knew I was in trouble. In the midst of my private agony, something told me that God loved me too much just to leave me alone in confusion. I found a passage in James that says, "If any of you lacks wisdom, he should ask God, who gives generously to all without finding fault, and it will be given to him" (1:5). I began to reconsider the whole issue. How could it be that God had given me a healthy sex drive at the age of twelve but forbade me from exploring it until I was married, probably ten years later, if I got married at all? What about wet dreams—how could God require people to control what happened while they were asleep? Furthermore, if everything was so clear-cut, why were there no Bible verses that said "Do not masturbate" the way they said "Do not commit adultery" and "Do not steal"?

I stopped assuming and started looking for answers. Is masturbation always wrong? Exactly what is it that makes it a sin? What I found was that there's a lot of disagreement about masturbation, even among the people who claim to know. Nobody has ever been able to give me the definitive answer to the question of masturbation. However, in the words of Jim Burns, a dedicated Christian author who has since become my close friend and mentor, I found the kind of understanding that many young people are looking for. In his excellent book on youth sexuality, *Handling Your Hormones*, I found this passage:

> If I must be pinned down, I believe that not all masturbation is necessarily sinful. However, you must make up your own mind. You must intelligently work through the decision. And I would suggest that you turn to God for help. Let me give you

two opposing viewpoints from two outstanding Christian people to help you arrive at your decision.

First, in his book *This Is Loving?* David Wilkerson says, "Masturbation is not a gift of God for the release of sex drives. Masturbation is not moral behavior and is not condoned in the Scriptures. . . . Masturbation is not harmless fun." On the other hand, Charlie Shedd, a much respected Christian authority on sex and dating, does call masturbation a "gift of God." He claims that masturbation "can be a positive factor in your total development" and goes on to say that "teenage masturbation is preferable to teenage intercourse. It is better to come home hot and bothered than satisfied and worried."

My own view is somewhere in between these two extremes. Masturbation is practically universal. It isn't the gross sin some people think it is, yet at times it can have a negative side to it.

Jim's book goes on to explain that masturbation becomes very negative when it becomes obsessive-compulsive and dominates a person's life and becomes sin when it involves uncontrolled fantasy and especially pornography or the semi-pornography that makes up so much of today's television.

I agree with him completely, especially on the last point. The most destructive things to me were and are the images that I have allowed to fill my mind through magazines, movies, and particularly television.

Beyond the images themselves, the modern media has a pornographic attitude toward sexuality, and women in particular, that reduces people to the status of objects and makes sex into a purely physical act. In the long run, though, television does something far worse than inspiring lust: it creates unrealistic expectations and false standards for young people.

Sex on television and in the movies almost always consists of first-time encounters between young, thin, beautiful people who aren't married to each other. Consequently, it comes across as unfailingly intense and exciting. These radiant Greek gods and goddesses never argue, pay bills, tend to screaming children, have a cold, get tired or depressed, or experience anything to cool their passions. They aren't real people, but watching them makes those of us who are married feel inadequate and gives those who are unmarried unrealistic expectations.

Married sex can be intense and exciting to be sure, but for different reasons and in different ways and not all the time. I used to think that parents who locked up the television and VCR were fuddy-duddies, but now I think that parents who don't are insane. Television is not just a problem for children, either. We all need to be aware of the not-so-subtle danger of letting a sick and often evil culture determine what we think about.

Paul said it well in Philippians 4:8: "Finally . . . whatever is true, whatever is noble, whatever is right, whatever is pure, whatever is lovely, whatever is admirable—if anything is excellent or praiseworthy—think about such things." Everything doesn't need to be "Christian" to fit that criteria, but we had better stop kidding ourselves about the effect of what we read and watch and think.

The point of all this, Dad, is that there was a lot going on with my sexuality that I needed help with, even before I got involved with actual relationships. I was very fortunate to be part of a very strong Christian support group in high school, and the love and trust there eventually allowed me to open up and share my struggles. I worry about people who suffer in silence—no one should have to work out their sexuality alone. I had you and Mom, too, and all of the things you described in your letter. As I said before, Dad, I always thought you neglected my sexual education. Now I see that in teaching me about love and relationships, you were giving me the most important lessons of all.

Love,

Bart

FIVE

MY FRIENDS, MY TEACHERS, AND OTHER ALIENS

Dear Dad,

I read a lot of books about parents and kids as I prepared to write these letters, Dad, and, frankly, it was a little discouraging. Ideas that had seemed so unique and creative when you and I discussed them turned out to be practically common knowledge after all, and I suddenly realized that we are not as brilliant as I thought we were (which means that we are *definitely* not as brilliant as you thought we were). As good as some of those books are, though, somehow it seems like a lot of them are based on the implicit assumption that if parents simply do their jobs right, their kids will automatically grow up into wonderful people; if they don't, their kids will surely be human disasters.

The general attitude seems to be that the family is some sort of closed system, operating in a vacuum. That kind of unspoken message bothers me because it clearly misunderstands the realities of the world today. The average kid experiences a whole host of teachers, coaches, counselors, babysitters, and grandparents before they are graduated from high school, not to mention the influences of their own friends and siblings, the church, and the mass media.

While I believe that you and Mom have done a terrific job as parents, the inescapable fact is that there are a lot of other people who have had a hand in making me into the person that I am, for better and for worse. Regardless of what anyone thinks of how I turned out, I am undeniably the product of a collaborative upbringing. You can't take all the credit—and more importantly, you can't shoulder all the blame. I've seen it happen too often to deny that a parent can single-handedly destroy a child, but I know that even two parents don't raise their children all by themselves. Too many other people impact our lives to allow it, and, for my money, that's usually a good thing.

Elsewhere in these letters, I write about how I became a Christian when I was fifteen years old. It's strange the way we Christians usually speak about becoming a Christian as though it were something we did once and were done with, like getting our tonsils taken out. In reality, accepting Jesus as Lord and Savior is just the first and easiest part of the lifelong task of becoming a Christian.

Even so, there is something very special about that first commitment that makes it a unique blessing. I've experienced some truly amazing things since I became a Christian, but I still don't think I will ever recapture the unbelievable excitement I had in those first weeks of my new life with God. Everything seemed so wonderful to me, and I couldn't believe my good fortune for being alive and full of faith. I can relate to the old hymn, "Amazing Grace" when it says, "How precious did that grace appear the hour I first believed," because I was a lonely, depressed kid looking to escape a life I hated when I was transformed by the overwhelming love of God, and becoming a Christian thrilled me.

New Christians are exciting people to be around, I think, because they don't take anything for granted, and they haven't yet learned to tone down their joy. They are often the most authentic Christians, too, because they take Jesus at his word when he says to love God with all your heart, soul, strength, and mind and to love your neighbor as yourself. Unfortunately, we who have been at it longer usually teach them to copy our own compromises instead of following their sense of commitment ourselves.

I spoke at a revival service not long ago in Northeast Philadelphia, and had the thrill of watching an older woman give her life to God. I would not have known about it, however, if her distraught daughter had not brought her up to talk with me after the service.

It seems that this woman had already begun to make plans for her new life in God's service and was considering leaving her job to work for a children's shelter downtown. Her daughter was very upset, primarily because she had been counting on her mother's income to finance a new boat. "Would you please tell my mom that being a Christian doesn't mean she should do everything for God?" the younger woman asked me. "If she quits her job, it's going to spoil everything."

Her mother looked at me with disappointed eyes and said sadly, "I thought she'd be happy for me, but all she keeps saying is that God doesn't expect us to go overboard. But he does, doesn't he?" We talked for fifteen minutes, and I encouraged the mother in her decision to follow God's calling no matter what, while her daughter fumed. I'm thankful that she was so full of excitement, and I can only hope that she got into fellowship with some other committed Christians and ignored the "kill-joy" she had raised.

As exciting as it is, the euphoria of salvation doesn't last forever. For me, it didn't last more than a few months. As my emotional commitment to God gradually subsided and I found myself unable to manufacture new doses of enthusiasm, I began to wonder if I really was a Christian after all or if I had simply gone on some sort of spiritual joyride that was about to end whether I wanted it to or not.

My friend Joel, who had led me to Christ, helped all he could, but he wasn't very much farther along than I was as a disciple. Neither were the rest of my newfound Christian friends, most of whom were "baby" Christians, just as I was. Like the seeds on the shallow soil in Jesus' parable of the sower, we had received the word with joy, but we had no roots. And like those same seeds, we were beginning to wither and die.

It was just about that time that a college student, Phil Thorne, took over our youth group. Although he was only twenty-one years old, Phil was not your average Christian college kid by any measure. He was married, for one thing, and he was also a top student at Haverford College, a highly academic secular school in our area. How he found the time to manage a youth group of well over 180 high school kids, I'll never know, but he did just that for more than a year, until the church hired a full-time youth pastor, and Phil stepped down to become a volunteer leader.

I was a sophomore in high school when Phil arrived, but already I was working hard as a part of the group's student leadership. Because our group was so big and our leaders were all part time, the kids did everything from planning events and recruiting to counseling and leading Bible studies. In a lot of ways it was a great thing for me to be able to jump right in and begin to put my newfound faith into action.

Before I knew it, I was doing a whole lot more than just setting up chairs and being part of a skit or two. By the time Phil arrived, I was clearly in a position of spiritual leadership—but with almost no biblical foundation and a faith that was fading fast. On the outside I probably looked like I had my act together, but on the inside I was one very uncertain young man.

Youth ministers talk a lot about relational ministry, which oftentimes simply means spending time with kids, and there's a lot to be said for being a friend to young people. But Phil approached me in a different way. After he introduced himself, he simply said, "You're Bart Campolo, and I hear you're pretty involved here. I'd like to have you and a few other guys get together with me once a week so I can help you grow in your relationship with God."

No frills. No inducements. He even set the time for our meetings at 6 a.m. on Tuesday mornings so as to weed out anyone who wasn't really committed to what he was trying to accomplish. Some people might say that he went about things all wrong, I suppose, but as a new Christian struggling to keep my faith alive, I didn't care much about the strategies of youth ministry. Here was someone who was willing to help me grow. I thought I had died and gone to heaven.

It would be hard to describe what Phil Thorne did for me over the next three years. To be sure, he taught me how to study the Bible, how to pray, and how to use my strengths as a person to influence other people for God, but he did more than just introduce me to the basics of Christianity. He made those Tuesday mornings a time when the other guys and I could talk about our lives honestly and work together to figure out what God wanted to do with us.

The conversations we had in Phil's living room were alive with the excitement of a group of boys who had found a man to lead them, and we talked for hours about everything from our girlfriends to predestination (I learned, by the way, that my girlfriend wasn't predestined to "dump" me, but she did anyway). We also grew close as friends because Phil showed us the way that Christians should care for one another in true fellowship. We weren't allowed to put each other down around him, because he knew that even playful put-downs can hurt and establish barriers between friends. We learned to pray for each other and keep each other in line, too.

I've made a lot of friends since that time, but I've never been part of any fellowship that had the kind of intensity and camaraderie that characterized what we ended up simply calling "The Group." When I got married years later, it was those guys—George, John, Rocky, Jeff, and Matthew, along with my college buddy Jerry—who stood up with me. Phil was at my wedding, too, because he was important to all of us, and we had become a part of his life.

Phil was much more than my teacher or even my Christian brother—he was my hero. To me, no one was smarter or handsomer or nicer or more in touch with God than he was. I tried to hide it from him, unsuccessfully I'm sure, but I wanted Phil's approval more than anything back then, and some of my happiest times were when he would take me along on an errand or let me help him with his laundry or tell me that I had done or said something well. One time he asked me to help him teach a few Sunday school classes, and I felt so honored that I must have walked on air for a week afterward.

I loved to be with him because of who he was and even more because I knew he cared about me even though he didn't have to. He asked me hard questions about myself, and he wasn't satisfied until I gave him straight answers. In answering Phil, I began to discover who I was and what my life was all about, or at least what I wanted it to be about. And I imitated him in every way I could think of because to me he was the greatest Christian man alive.

As I am writing all of this down and thinking about that time in my life, it occurs to me that it must have been awfully hard on you to see me respond that way to someone else. All of a sudden, another man was at the center of my life, where you had always been. It wasn't just that I devoted so much time to my little support group and to the larger youth group as well. All of a sudden I was full of new ideas and perspectives, and I measured everything, including my family, by the things I was learning from Phil. I'm sure you got tired of hearing "Phil says . . ." or "Well, according to Phil . . ." over and over again, but you never said a word about it to me. Here you were, my own father, preaching and teaching young people all over the country about the Christian life, and your own son was somebody else's disciple, not because you had walked out on me or let me down somehow, but rather because I had turned to Phil instead of you.

I've been a youth worker myself since that time, and sometimes kids respond in that same way to me. It amazes me because I know I'm not half the person my young followers make me out to be, and I try not to let their praise affect my self-concept. It is all too easy for those kids to put me on a pedestal—they only see me in short doses when I'm at my best and in an environment they love. They don't get a chance to see my weaknesses the same way they see those of their parents. Often my only job is to care for their emotional and spiritual needs and give them a good time, while their parents have to deal with all the nitty-gritty stuff of their daily lives. Phil had that same advantage with me, of course, but I didn't know it at the time. So he was my hero, and you were just my dad, and I feel very sure that I let you know that every chance I could.

Although I know I must have hurt you, Dad, you never did a thing to undermine what was happening in my life. On the contrary, you encouraged it. There was never any battle for my allegiance because you never put up a fight or said a single word against Phil or anything he taught me—even when those things conflicted with your own thinking and beliefs.

If you had wanted to, I feel sure that you could have found a weakness in my Phil-inspired belief system, or in my image of Phil himself, and used it to make me turn away from him, but you didn't do anything like that. You kept quiet, even when I spouted off with the self-righteous judgments that new Christians are so prone to mistake for wisdom, and you supported what was going on in my life even though I almost completely left you out of it. You could have tried to hold onto me or make me feel guilty about leaving you behind, but instead you let me go.

I am fully convinced now that nothing you could have done at that time would have been as good for me as what you didn't do. I was finally growing, and more than anything in the world, I needed to grow on my own just then.

There are a lot of reasons why I left you out, of course. Both as an adolescent and as a new Christian, I was establishing my own identity, and while I wasn't exactly rebelling against you, I didn't want that identity to become nothing more than an extension of your own. Maybe some people would say that I had something to prove, but I think it had more to do with my knowledge that you were too powerful a person for me to handle at that point. You have a way of expressing your opinions that makes them seem like facts, and I knew that I would never be able to stand up to you in a discussion or an argument. Phil was powerful, too, but he was my friend and my choice, so I didn't resent his efforts to shape my personality. You, however, were someone who could have taken away my individuality altogether.

If I let you in, I told myself, I would gradually become just like you and lose myself in the process. I was afraid that your relationship to God would become my relationship to God, and even at that point in my growth I instinctively knew that that kind of thing was the ultimate danger.

Jesus had died so that I could have my own direct relationship with God, even if it was weak and sporadic and filled with doubts and fears. It belonged to me, and I wasn't taking any chances on losing it by mixing it up with you.

Besides, I didn't want you to know about a lot of the stuff I was dealing with just then. Like most boys that age, I was essentially a walking hormone factory, and it immediately became clear to me that my survival as a Christian had a lot to do with sorting out my sexuality. Unfortunately, that wasn't an issue you and I openly discussed. Amazingly enough, the guys in my support group eventually trusted each other enough to talk about our sexual lives, our struggles with pornography and lust and even masturbation, and to hold each other accountable as brothers in Christ. But even when I admitted that stuff to them, Dad, there was no way I was going to admit it to you.

I was also very proud and excited about the things that my support group was accomplishing as a ministry team in our high school. Phil insisted that, while Bible study, prayer, and personal piety (keeping ourselves straight as far as sex, drugs, language, etc., were concerned) were all vital, we could never grow the way God wanted us to if we weren't out in the world acting as his servants. Before long Phil had us sharing the Gospel with our friends, leading prayer groups during lunch at school, inviting people to our youth group, and planning special events that were aimed at sharing the love of God by creating a warm atmosphere of friendship. As we worked together, God used us at our high school to draw people to him.

It was really exciting for us to be leading some of our friends to Christ and seeing God work in their lives. Next to some of the things that you were involved with, Dad, the work that we were doing seemed pretty insignificant. I would come home from a Bible study all thrilled because one kid had shown an interest in what I'd said, but after I heard about the rally where you had spoken to 10,000 people and had seen 500 give their lives to Jesus, it just didn't seem worth mentioning. You were building orphanages while I was trying to witness to my basketball coach. You were writing theology while I was figuring out who all of Jesus' 12 disciples were. It's not that I resented what you were doing—I was proud then, just as I'm proud now, and excited about the way God was using you—but it made me feel small to think about placing my stories next to yours, so I didn't. I've had variations of that feeling throughout my life, and no doubt will until the day I die. I know that we're not supposed to compare ourselves with other people, but it's awfully hard not to do it just the same.

Lately, though, I've discovered that God doesn't see things quite the way I do. What impresses him is not the end result of an action, but the purity of the motives and the quality of faithfulness that go into it. As Mother Teresa put it, "God has not called us to be successful—he has called us to be faithful to him." By that measure, those early efforts were probably my finest because I hadn't yet grown skillful and polished, and I relied solely on the power of God. All of the training seminars and experience I've had since then have certainly made me a more capable and seasoned minister, but I often think I was better off when I hadn't yet developed so much confidence in myself.

Jesus said, "If a man remains in me and I in him, he will bear much fruit; apart from me you can do nothing" (John 15:5), but I still find myself trying to do all sorts of things in my own strength. To God, though, the only ministry that really counts is that which is accomplished by his power. When we are willing to empty ourselves of our own desires and motivations and allow him to do his will through us, then our ministry will have power. The things I did in high school belonged to him that way, and that means they were very important. I know now that you would have seen them that way if I had shared them with you, Dad. But as exciting as they were to me, I tended to hold them back from you then because—in my mind—they didn't measure up.

I guess I should feel apologetic about having left you out of my spiritual life for so long at that point, but I don't. It was important for me to develop my own relationship with God, and that's exactly what happened. Maybe I would feel differently, though, if you hadn't offered yourself to me all over again when I began to lose my bearings in college. By then I had developed enough confidence in myself that I didn't fear being overpowered, and it felt good when you began to talk with me as though I were your Christian brother as well as your son. Your spiritual guidance has meant a lot to me since then, and I've come to know you in a way I never could have imagined as a boy. You waited for me, though, and let God use someone else in my life, and that made all the difference in the world.

A lot of new Christians don't last very long because they have no one like Phil to help them put down roots and grow. Clearly that means something has gone very wrong with Christian leadership. I don't mean to sound cynical, but it seems that a lot of evangelism being done today is actually worse for the people we reach than if we had left them alone. Once they make a decision for Christ, that is exactly what we do—leave them alone. It is no wonder that so few of them actually survive as disciples. When the Apostle Peter says of such people that "It would have been better for them not to have known the way of righteousness, than to have known it and then to turn their backs on the sacred command that was passed on to them" (2 Peter 2:21), we who cavalierly lead others to Christ and then make no provision for their continued growth should shudder with fear. We would be kinder to keep our Good News to ourselves unless we can provide the kind of support that will give a new Christian a fighting chance.

I know so many people who have sprung up quickly as believers only to have their faith wither and die because there was no one to come alongside them and help them put down roots. That's not just a shame; it's a sin. Everywhere I look, and especially in the ghettos where I work, there is a need for mature Christians who will offer themselves as mentors and friends to kids, and especially to Christian kids who are struggling to live for God.

God brought Phil Thorne into my life and used his example and his love to inspire me and to make me strong. I love Phil with my whole heart and am forever thankful for him and to him.

Nothing could have happened, though, Dad, if you hadn't let it happen, and for that I am every bit as thankful. You had to step into the background for a time, and you did it graciously, humbly, and unselfishly. I know you loved me then because you did what was best for me instead of what was best for you.

Of course, you didn't let just anyone become my role model unchallenged. The reason I know that you could have undermined Phil in my eyes if you had wanted to is that you did just that to some other people when you felt their influence on me was negative. Like most kids growing up, I was always being impressed by somebody, and my personality changed nearly as quickly as my role models did. As with my peers, though, you kept a close eye on my heroes.

A few years before I became a Christian, I had a teacher in school who quickly convinced me that he knew everything in the world worth knowing. He was a quick-witted cynic, and I thought he was the coolest man alive. When I began to parrot his words and ideas the way I did later on with Phil's, however, you weren't so passive. Oh, you knew better than to ridicule or contradict my reigning role model directly, for that would have only increased my loyalty by offending my sense of fair play. Since he was not there to face your attacks, I would have become his defender. So instead of a frontal assault, you and Mom developed a far more effective approach.

Instead of downplaying my hero, both of you became very interested in whatever it was he said each day. But the questions you asked to draw me out were also designed to make me follow my teacher's way of thinking through to its conclusions. For instance, when I repeated a saucy joke that he'd made about women, you didn't get upset. You simply said, "I wonder how you would feel if that had been your mother he was talking about, or your sister?" and left me to figure out the obvious answer. Humor that degrades women never seems so funny when you think about women as real people instead of sexual objects, so I didn't much like the joke when I thought of it that way. It felt wrong.

Another time it was his perspective on the welfare system and another time his statements about the importance of athletics, but always you asked questions that forced me to look beyond my teacher's clever words to the basically selfish attitudes that lay behind them. You didn't put him down exactly, but you didn't let his influence get very far either.

Once you had sown the seeds of doubt, though, it was Mom who finished him off as a role model. He wasn't the kind of man she liked, I knew, but she didn't try to make me dislike him myself. She knew a better way to stop his influence over me. As you began to expose the gaps in my hero's armor, she tried to make me feel sorry for him instead of angry.

"That poor man," she lamented, "he must have had awful trouble in his life to make him feel that way. You should do your best to be kind to him, Bart. I think he needs some kindness to soften his heart." She was right about my teacher, I think, but that was not the only reason she said what she did. You both knew that if I began to pity this man, he was finished as a role model. And so it was that I came to really care for that teacher and yet came to no harm in the process.

It was inevitable that I would look to other people besides you for guidance and examples, and I think you always knew that. But even if you couldn't be my only influence, you saw to it that no one got a clear shot at me unless it was for my good. I've had more than my share of significant adults, some of whom I am convinced you actually coerced into my life to help me, and I've been affected just as profoundly by some of my peers over the years. Each of them has touched my life and my character in some way, and in them, I see the hands of God shaping me into the person he wants me to be.

Without a doubt, you and Mom have exerted the greatest influence, though, and one of the most significant ways you have done that is by allowing, encouraging, and interpreting all of those other people in my life. You didn't do all the work on this temple of God, but you had a major role in determining who did.

All of this writing about role models and teachers reminds me of one of the last things Phil showed me in the Bible before I graduated from high school. In 2 Timothy 2:1–2, the Apostle Paul gives a specific charge to his disciple Timothy. "You then, my son, be strong in the grace that is in Christ Jesus. And the things you have heard me say in the presence of many witnesses entrust to reliable men who will also be qualified to teach others." After Phil read that passage aloud, he looked at me and said, "Bart, I've put a lot of myself into you, and I love you. Now I expect you to do the same for someone else. That is the way of Christ, and that must be our way as well."

He was right, of course; personal discipleship is the way of Christ. I suppose there's a place for television evangelism and video Bible studies, and I enjoy Christian concerts and festivals a great deal, but those are not the ways that Jesus made his disciples. Disciples are made through an intentional relationship with a mature Christian—someone who celebrates our victories and points out our areas of weakness—someone who sometimes gives us the answers and at other times makes us ask the questions—someone who prays for us and with us—and someone who ultimately refuses to let us slip away from God without a fight. All of those other things that make up the Christian subculture are fine, so long as buildings, programs, and paraphernalia don't get in the way or become so important to us that we fail to establish the kinds of personal relationships that bring about true Christian growth. What's the use of all our churches, choirs, evangelistic outreaches, books of theology, and everything else if we are only making believers—and not disciples—out of all men and women?

Don't get me wrong, Dad. You know that I'm not some radical who's out to undermine organized Christianity. I believe in the Church. I moved back to Philadelphia and started Kingdom Builders Supply specifically to work with inner-city churches.

KBS brings solid inner-city churches that are committed to neighborhood ministry together with Christian college students and adults who need vision and the chance to make a difference with their lives. We help those churches design effective summer outreach programs, and then we recruit teams of full-time summer volunteers from around the country to make those programs happen. The organization is based on a fairly simple premise: inner-city churches are the last, best hope for people in our nation's ghettos. What we're doing, though, is more than just empowering those churches for the work God has called them to do. By using college students as volunteers, we're also inspiring a new generation of young people to service and discipleship among the poor.

A typical KBS summer program includes things like day camps for children, evening youth groups, community cleanup days, neighborhood Bible studies, Christian block parties, and lots of visitation. It's hard, but it's a lot of fun, too. Volunteers don't experience only poverty and injustice; they also feel the joy of being used by God to meet needs. That's the kind of experience that changed my life, and it can change their lives as well. The real goal of KBS is to challenge people not only to a summer, but also to a whole lifetime of service. Inner-city churches need more than short-term volunteers to build the Kingdom of God amid the desperation and desolation of their neighborhoods. They need committed Christian disciples who are dedicated to nurturing more committed Christian disciples.

That's what churches everywhere need, I think. We can't simply offer people the Gospel and expect them to survive unless we also offer them relationships with mature Christians who will help them to grow. That really is the way of Christ, and it must be our way as well. I guess I got a little carried away there, Dad, but I know that you'll understand. This stuff is important to me.

Every child, every person is sacred because he or she is made in the image of God and is a place where God desires to dwell. I want to do all I can to see to it that more kids, and especially poor kids, have a chance to have relationships that can help them to grow in their relationships to God and become the people he intends for them to be.

I'm glad that you let me have the kind of relationship I had with Phil. I'm glad I have that same kind of relationship with you now. I hope that throughout my life, and especially in my work with Kingdom Builders Supply, I'll be able to provide those kinds of relationships for other people. The world doesn't need any more nominal believers, but it desperately needs more disciples of Jesus Christ.

Love,

Bart

*   *   *   *

Dear Bart,

Thanks for your letter. It very much confirmed the old cliché that if you want to hold onto somebody, you must learn to let them go. When you moved into your teens I was well aware of what every parent must know, and that is that an adolescent boy must establish his identity over and against that of his father. The same thing is true for mothers and daughters. Every normal kid comes to that point when he or she has to say, "I'm not you! I'm me!" That statement can best be made when there is somebody other than a parent who can provide a model of what that kid would like to be. The time came when you knew you had to be your own self. There was that psychological need to construct an identity different from mine. Even as you faced that task, you were well aware that you could not construct this new identity out of nothing. It was only natural that you should look around and try to construct the new you out of building materials that were readily available in your social world.

Thank God that Phil Thorne was there when you were doing all of this. He was not me, but he was committed to the same Jesus that I love. He had a different kind of personality and a different perspective on how the Christian life should be lived. Nevertheless, he loved you and wanted you to be all that Jesus had called you to be. That you found Phil, or that he found you, was a great relief to me. In the end, I feel sure it was God who arranged for you to meet each other as an answer to my prayers that you would be protected from Satan and his workers. I am thankful to God that you did not resist the relationship with Phil, which I know is largely responsible for your stance in Christ today.

Of course, it was a little hard on me to have a theology and lifestyle prescribed by someone else become dominant for you. Certainly there was some mild irritation on my part at being judged by whatever came out of Phil's mouth. I remember the day you questioned my devotional life because I wasn't reading my Bible and praying with the kind of faithfulness that Phil had prescribed. What was even worse was that Phil was right, and I had to stand corrected by his judgment coming from you. There was even some jealousy associated with seeing how your new-found hero was impacting your life. I suppose if a man can't handle such things, he is far too insecure to be a good father, and he ought to get some counseling on how to be an adult.

What you didn't mention in your letter was that Phil was the youth leader in a church that was different from the one attended by the rest of our family. Getting involved with him and with his youth group meant that on Sundays you went to church without us. Looking back on your high school years, I'm glad that we had the sense to let you go. I think Mom was most affected by your decision. She often wondered if it was okay to split up the family like that. There was even some consideration given to the whole family changing churches. Other families whose kids had been reached by Phil's ministry and whose kids wanted to be a part of his youth group had made that kind of move.

Personally, I think parents are crazy if they don't identify with a church that turns their kids on spiritually. I could never quite figure out how in some parents' minds denominational loyalty takes precedence over the spiritual well-being of their children. Providing a meaningful church experience for kids may be one of the most important tasks for parents of teenagers.

In our case, we didn't change churches, but we let you change. We figured that being in a church apart from ours would be a good thing for a kid like you. Too often you had to labor under the weight of being Tony Campolo's son, and being in a church outside of my sphere of influence gave you a chance to develop as a Christian and become a leader without having my shadow looming over you.

As a teenager, you chose Phil, but earlier in your life I often chose those who would act as role models for you and who would exercise influence over you. When you were a little boy, I gave very careful consideration to whom our family would visit and who would be invited to visit us in our home.

At the top of the list was my mother. We visited her often, and you had lots of fun times at her house. My mom was a great storyteller, and most of all she was great at relating the history of the Campolo family. I could count on her to relate the exploits of my youth and to make me look bigger than life. It always surprises me that more grandparents don't grasp that helping their grandchildren to understand their roots and background is one of their primary responsibilities. Your

Mom-Mom Campolo was committed to making you sense that you were part of a great family tradition and that it was your responsibility to carry on with honor.

Mom-Mom knew that telling a good story required a certain degree of embellishment and that the reality was never quite as dramatic as she made it out to be. Oral tradition is never pure history; it is far more important than that. The story of a family should always be a glorious tale that is left unfinished so as to invite the young to write new chapters that are worthy of what has gone before. There ought to be a law that prohibits grandparents from running away to Florida in retirement! They should not be allowed to escape from their responsibility to build a sense of family continuity and tradition into their grandchildren. There also ought to be a law that requires parents to regularly take their children to see grandparents so that those who are old can tell those who are young the story of the family! This is crucial if children are to know who they are and what they ought to be.

Both Mom and I put a lot of thought into deciding whom we would invite into our home when you and Lisa were young, being well aware of how impressionable kids are. I was on the faculty of the University of Pennsylvania during the time that Penn had a nationally ranked basketball team. You and all your classmates looked up to these players as superstars. I had some members of the team as students in one of my seminar classes and had come to know them as friends outside of class, so I made sure to invite them to visit us. They were neat guys who treated me with respect and made it clear that there was more to life than basketball. The fact that people you admired thought highly of your parents may have had a lot to do with how you came to view us.

Sociologists in the field of the family have long known of the influence of visitors on the character formation of children, and prominent scholars among them have urged that parents give more attention to who comes and does not come into a child's home. I often recall the story of the way in which a missionary who visited in the home of George Seagraves when he was a boy altered the future of his life. His parents had invited the missionary to have dinner with their family on a Sunday afternoon. After the meal was over, the missionary played with young George for several hours and climaxed their pleasant afternoon by drinking a glass of water while standing on his head. Seeing this "awesome feat" left the boy with an inescapable desire to be a missionary, too. Years later, George Seagraves became a world-famous missionary in Burma, saved countless lives, and led many to know Christ. Such are the consequences of outside influences on children. Parents may not provide all of the major influences that work themselves out in the lives of their children, but they can certainly help to determine who does provide them. In the end that may be the most important influence of all.

Love,

Dad

SIX

COLLEGE: WHERE IT ALL COMES TOGETHER OR IT ALL FALLS APART

Dear Bart,

I really tried to get you to go to a Christian college rather than a secular school. Having been a professor of sociology in both kinds of colleges, I was acutely aware of what can happen to impressionable students during four years of higher education. It was one of my greatest fears that some awe-inspiring professor, whose cynicism would make him seem all the more worldly wise, would make Christianity seem like an archaic folk religion to you.

When I was on the faculty of the University of Pennsylvania, I had the chance to observe firsthand several students who started their college training as believers, only to turn into cynics who scoffed at the Christian faith and derided those who held onto their beliefs, as though they belonged to the Flat Earth Society. One day I was discussing religion with one of those students, and I was stunned by the bitter contempt she had toward anything Christian. I can still hear her saying, "I don't know how my parents could have drilled all of that crap into my head."

"Maybe it was because they loved you," I responded. "And maybe it was because they wanted you to know the truth."

"Don't tell me that you believe all of that stuff!" she inquired with an air of heightened disbelief. "How can you accept all those wild Bible stories? How can a person smart enough to know better believe in the Bible?"

My answer to her was simple and direct: "I decided to! And why *don't* you believe in the Bible and its message of salvation?

Isn't it because you decided to reject it? Don't tell me that some-body *proved* to you that the Bible was a pack of fairy tales or that Jesus was never crucified and resurrected from the grave to pro-vide us with salvation. I know better than that. Isn't the real rea-son that you have decided to turn your back on the Christian faith tied up in the fact that it's not cool to be a believer in aca-demia? Isn't your real reason for turning your back on Jesus due to your fear that your profs might think you a bit quaint and that your fellow students might consider you somewhat unso-phisticated?

"Come on," I said to her, "tell the truth. Honest doubt I respect, but when a person turns away from Jesus primarily because being a Christian doesn't go with the version of open-mindedness that has come to be considered the mark of hav-ing been educated, I can only bite my tongue and try not to sneer."

In retrospect, I think I was a bit cruel with her, but I do hope that I got her thinking about the real reasons why she said that she no longer believed in the biblical revelation. College pro-fessors are often worshiped by students, especially if those students are endeavoring to establish distance between them-selves and their parents in the process of going through some kind of late adolescent rebellion. A charismatic professor can provide legitimization for rejecting what religious parents are all about. Identifying with some academic gadfly who makes Christianity seem like a cross between superstition and mili-taristic racism can enable such young people to think of them-selves as superior to old mom and dad and to believe that they have moved beyond the seeming naïveté of their parents.

When I taught at a secular university, I became very aware of how powerful an influence a professor can have over stu-dents. In my case, I was able to make having faith appear as a brave and courageous thing. I could set up the arguments in classroom discussions so that not to believe in God made life totally absurd and without any moral basis. I doubt if I made many converts, but to my students Christianity usually became a viable option for a legitimate world-view.

A couple of years ago, I was walking down the Avenue of the Americas in New York City when a young woman came running up to me exclaiming, "Dr. Campolo! Dr. Campolo! Do you remember me? I had you for Intro to Sociology at Penn. I want you to know," she went on to say, "that the course you taught was an incredible experience for me. That whole year I really believed in God." Such is the power of some of the men and women who serve as college profs. No wonder James the apostle wrote:

> Not many of you should presume to be teachers, my brothers, because you know that we who teach will be judged more strictly.
>
> *James 3:1, MV*

For those who use the position of academic leadership to destroy faith while playing games that feed their own egos, I can only mention the words of Jesus:

> But whoso shall offend one of these little ones which believe in me, it were better for him that a millstone were hanged about his neck, and that he were drowned in the depth of the sea.
>
> *Matthew 18:6*

A Christian college can do much more than just provide professors who can be role models for faith. This is not to minimize the fact that having Christian teachers in some of your most formative years can play a major part in your faith formation, but there is another important reason for taking your college training at a Christian college; namely, the development of a Christian world-view. There are some who still argue that information is neutral and that truth is objective. But ever since scholars began probing the phenomenology of knowledge, there has been an increasingly accepted postulate that information is always selected and arranged to support a particular point of view. There is a growing awareness that the subjective commitments of the knower determine how reality is understood and what truth appears to be. It is not that objective truth does not exist, but rather that the personal convictions of the knower determine how that objective truth is handled and understood.

What all this means is that what a college student is taught is inevitably made to support a particular point of view. At a Christian college, you would have learned to look at things the way Christians do. You would have learned biology in a way that would have affirmed belief in a Creator. You would have learned psychology in a way that would have had you view human beings as moral creatures, responsible for their actions and ultimately answerable to God. In the arts, you would have been focused on the religious concerns that gave birth to the music of Bach and the paintings of Michelangelo. You would have discovered that even the existential concerns of secular artists probe ultimate questions that can only be resolved in faith. In short, your entire approach to the world would have been shaped by the Christian faith so that what you learned and what the Bible teaches would be integrated into a unified system of knowledge.

In Christian colleges that remain true to their original purposes, all education supports the theme that Christ is Lord of all. Therefore, in the study of sociology, economics, and political science, there should be an underlying commitment to social justice. The task is not simply to understand the world, but to figure out how to transform it into the kind of world that Jesus wants it to be—in other words, into the Kingdom of God. At its best, the Christian college is not a greenhouse for the safe growth of kids who need protection from the big, bad world, but a boot camp for those who would join a movement that will triumph in history.

Secular universities no longer seem to me to have any real commitment to answering the ultimate questions of human existence such as "Where did we come from?" "Where are we going?" "Why are we here?" As Allan Bloom so strongly contends in his book, *The Closing of the American Mind*, secular universities no longer have any sense of mission or purpose other than that of providing vocational training for those who want to climb the ladders of economic and social success. They have been transformed into the ideal incubators for would-be yuppies. Bart, the last thing in the world I wanted for you to be was a yuppie. They seem so boring!

There is one other concern that I had about the college you would attend. A large percentage of those who attend college find their mates there. I wanted you to marry a Christian woman, and I knew that if you attended a Christian school your chances of marrying a Christian would be greatly enhanced. This might seem a bit devious, but it is the hidden agenda for many of us who have tried to guide our kids to Christian colleges—and, what's more, it's a strategy that often works.

But you didn't fall in line with what I wanted you to do. I guess I can't blame you. For years we lived on the campus of Eastern College, where I teach, and I realized long before you made your decision about college that you wanted to sample a different environment. Nevertheless, I did what a parent is supposed to do when trying to get a kid like you turned on to a Christian college: I had you visit the ones I thought would interest you. I sent you to Wheaton, because I felt that there you would find the smartest student body. I sent you to Calvin College because I thought that there you would find the sharpest faculty. I sent you to Furman University because I believed that there you would find a Christian atmosphere which transcended the legalisms that often haunt Christian schools. In the end, you chose Haverford College, a secular school with a Quaker tradition and extremely high academic expectations.

It was interesting to learn why you chose Haverford. You told me that it was because of what the students there talked about during their off hours. The conversations in the dining hall and the student lounges seemed to you to be filled with exciting discussions about world concerns and the urgent issues of the day. In your observations, the talk among students on Christian college campuses seemed trivial by comparison. Regretfully, I have to agree with you. I, too, have noticed the difference, but I think you were judging Christian college students against students of the highest academic caliber that secular schools had to offer. If you had visited most of the state universities and community colleges that I have visited on my speaking tours, you might have thought better of Christian colleges. Nonetheless, it does seem a bit strange to me that students at Christian colleges don't seem more mature. There is a high-schoolish quality in the dispositions of many of them when it comes to academic affairs and social concerns. Perhaps it's because those of us who run Christian colleges tend to treat our students as something less than adults. In any case, I found it difficult to argue with you.

Still, I wish you had gone to a Christian college because I am convinced that there is much more to a college education than academics. At Eastern, for instance, there is a concerted effort to get students involved in ministry. Tutoring programs for ghetto kids, prison ministries, and a variety of Christian groups like Evangelicals for Social Action are aimed at getting our undergraduates involved in meeting the needs of the poor and oppressed. Most other Christian colleges make similar efforts to get their students off campus and into the kind of transforming experiences that privileged kids can have only when they reach out to minister to those who suffer. I believe that college students can only have good minds if they have "dirty hands"—and I wanted you to have "dirty hands" as you worked in the kinds of difficult places where good Christian colleges try to place their students.

The first year at Haverford College didn't seem to go well for you. You failed to be the flashy soccer star you had been in high school; you and the coach never hit it off very well. While most of your classes went well, your work in science courses and your failure to master computers made you something less than a complete success. I think that a lot of kids who are accustomed to easy triumphs in high school experience something of a psychological shock when they discover that they are rather average at a first-rate college. While I know it happens to a lot of kids, it was a particularly painful thing for me to see my own kid going through this adjustment. You didn't seem to handle it all that well. You became strange and difficult to talk to. The old happy-go-lucky Bart was gradually slipping away, and a rather morose new kid seemed to be taking his place.

You were no longer in close contact with the gang you ran with in high school. Those church kids who had formed a close-knit fellowship built on mutual concern and support were no longer part of your daily experience. You were cut off from the land of spiritual renewal that comes from intimate

Christian friends who are there to keep you spiritually faithful and morally straight. The loss of this influence on your life was fairly obvious, and I prayed long hours that the Lord would provide some new means of renewing and sustaining your faith in Christ.

Then came one of my biggest frights. There seemed to me to be some hints that you might be homosexual. Looking back on it now, the whole set of circumstances seems ridiculous. But Haverford College had an attraction for homosexuals. The Quaker tradition of the school had generated an openness and acceptance of people whom society had long persecuted. The administration and faculty of the college had worked hard to overcome the homophobia that seems so rampant in our society. As a consequence of these attitudes and actions, Haverford had become a place where homosexuals could feel at home. You talked about the homosexual behavior of some of the guys in your dorm and how you had unintentionally walked in on some embarrassing and intimate situations in the normal course of your dorm living. The new sullenness that was very uncharacteristic of the old you suggested that something was troubling you. Then you started to wear an earring, which in some circles is interpreted as a sign of a homosexual identity. One day when you were home, you wanted to borrow Mom's nail polish remover. We didn't know what for, but when parents are filled with fear, every little thing gets misinterpreted.

I had always tried to teach you that for most people sexual orientation is not a choice. I had tried to explain to you as you were growing up that those who persecute homosexuals—sometimes under religious auspices—are often ignorant of the fact that, in the overwhelming number of cases, whatever biological and sociological factors have imprinted our homosexual brothers and sisters occurred long before there was any self-awareness of what was going on in their lives. Furthermore, I had pointed out that many homosexuals who become Christians still maintain their homosexual orientations and choose lives of celibacy as the primary way to continue life in the evangelical community. I had tried to teach you to respect and love those people who have suffered so much at the hands of uninformed and cruel people. I had preached compassion and understanding of homosexuals. Now, however, the issue was no longer hypothetical for me. It was existential.

Was my kid a homosexual? If so, how would I react? What if I found out you had a homosexual lover? Would I continue to love you as I had told so many parents of homosexual kids to do? Would I be able, in any way, to accept your homosexual lover—even if I believed intellectually that as a Christian I should love him regardless of what my religious upbringing had taught me on this matter? You'll never know the hours I walked the floors alone, praying and thinking and working through all of these questions.

In spite of knowing better, I did all the things a typical parent in my place would do. I frequently inquired about your dating life and probably would have welcomed the news that you had gotten sexually involved with some young woman. That's how crazy a so-called enlightened parent can be driven by latent homophobia. Perhaps you remember that I finally had to ask you outright—and I will never forget you answering—"Dad, I'm too heterosexual for my own good!" I sighed a sigh of relief—and then I began to worry about what was implied in that statement. Such are the worries of fathers!

During your second year at Haverford, I felt that I had to do something to rescue you from what I interpreted as spiritual slippage. I wondered whether the liberal theologies you were learning in your religion classes were taking their toll on you. I wondered if, as a consequence, you were becoming cold toward Christianity with all of its moral expectations. Regardless of what might be going on, I was aware that something precious was dying inside you and that something needed to be done to revive you spiritually.

About that time, Glenn Welch, the pastor of a small Methodist church near your college, contacted me and asked if I knew of anybody who would be interested in working with his youth group, and I recommended you. You decided to take the job, and you were great! You got right into your ministry with renewed zeal, and in no time at all, you seemed to once again be alive in Christ. I am convinced that getting involved in Christian service is one sure way to foster spiritual renewal in a college kid. I know it worked with you. Between your ministry with youth and the wise counsel of Glenn, a bright and confident Bart once again began to emerge.

Still, all was not well. At the end of your sophomore year at Haverford, you asked if you could take some time off from school. Part of your reasoning had to do with your renewed commitment to ministry. It bothered you that we were spending so much money on your education when there were so many needs out there in the world. You realized that, like so many college students, you were in college only because you couldn't think of anything better to do. Your awareness of the staggering needs in places like Haiti, the Dominican Republic, and Camden, New Jersey, made you think it would be best if you got right to work.

It took some persuading, but you finally convinced me that this would be a good thing. A lot of parents get scared when their kids want to take time off from college and fear that they might never return to finish their education. Looking back on it now, I think that taking time off was a very good thing for you. A lot of college kids haven't the slightest clue as to what they are supposed to be getting out of college. They graduate from high school and are expected to go to college—and so they do. It might have been a good idea if we had given you the chance to take some time off after high school so that you could catch your breath and try to figure out what your life was supposed to be all about. We parents sometimes rush our kids through stages of growth and development when they would be better off passing through them at their own pace. There are times when it is a good thing to let kids come up for air and get their bearings.

It was the end of the summer when we decided that you should take some time off from school. We were fortunate in that it was possible for you to travel and work along with me for a few months. You even enrolled in one of my classes at Eastern. Day in and day out, we were together. We talked, exchanged ideas, and learned a lot about each other. You were battling your way to your own identity, and it was a good thing to watch. That was a precious time for me because it was a rare opportunity to get to know my son as the emerging adult who was gradually becoming a partner in ministry.

When you decided to return to school, you had two reasons: you realized that there were some things you needed to know that you could learn in college and you understood that to be able to best help the poor and disadvantaged, you would need the kind of credentials that would merit respect from those who could provide support for your ministry.

You decided that you would take your last two years at Brown University. I wondered how you would ever be accepted because at that time, Brown was the hardest school in the country to get into, and its attitude toward transfer students was less than inviting. I thought that if they gave you an interview and looked at your high SAT scores, you would have a pretty good chance. Fortunately, we had a friend with enough influence to get you the interview, and the rest is, as they say, history. Influence can't make a person a success, but it can certainly position that person to take advantage of a chance for success if he or she has what it takes.

I often wonder about all the great kids who have what it takes but never get positioned to show their stuff. In a truly just society, everybody would have the chance to be all that they could be—but it's not a fair world, and it wasn't fair with you. You had some extra things going for you that a lot of other kids don't.

From the beginning, life at Brown went well for you. It wasn't but a few days after you arrived on campus that you made contact with some fellow students who were in Campus Crusade for Christ, a Christian organization that was in high gear on Brown's campus. They swept you into their fellowship, and before long, you were leading Bible study groups and sharing your convictions about Christ with others. There was marked growth in your Christian character. When your involvements with Christians led to your getting involved with a ministry in the ghetto of Providence, Rhode Island, I knew that things would be all right for you. I felt relieved. My prayers were being answered.

What I learned from all of this is that attending a secular school can be a time of spiritual growth and service, providing the right contacts are made with fellow students. You never seemed to find the Christian fellowship you needed at

Haverford. I know there were good Christians on campus, but for reasons that I do not know, you never seemed to gel with them.

Becoming a vital part of a circle of Christian friends at Brown, however, made all the difference in the world for you. I think that when parents look at the secular schools that their children might attend, they should give special attention to whether or not there is a dynamic Christian group on campus that could provide spiritual nurturance and challenges. There is no guarantee that their children will plug into such groups, but being sure that they exist is the least that parents should consider.

Organizations like InterVarsity Christian Fellowship, Navigators, and Campus Crusade for Christ have chapters on many secular campuses. At some colleges, like Duke University, the chaplain has put together relational groups that keep students alive and growing. Sometimes denominational programs (like the Wesley Foundation at Texas Tech) provide the context for Christian life and witness. After seeing what happened to you at Brown, I wish I had done more investigating as to who was doing what for Christ on campus before the decision was made as to where you would do your college work.

All in all, you came through college in pretty good shape. You took good courses and did a lot of thinking and an awful lot of growing. If I have any real criticism to lend it is that I don't think you took enough advantage of extracurricular activities. When you were at Haverford, you could have made the basketball team, but you didn't even try out. Perhaps you were afraid to or perhaps you were overreacting to me and my wishes for you. I don't know, but I wish you had. I wish you had gone out for the school paper or student government or something. Nevertheless, you came through college a Christian—and a better one at that. So I had better count my blessings and be proud of what you did become by God's grace and through a lot of hard work on your part.

Love,

Dad

*   *   *   *

Dear Dad,

You and I will probably never agree about all of this college
stuff, but for the record, I think I had better register my version
of the story even though I don't expect to change your mind.
On the one hand, you have taught at a Christian college for
more than twenty years now, so it would be pretty disap-
pointing to me if you didn't take that side of the argument. On
the other hand, it just may be that your loyalty to Christian
higher education keeps you from seeing the other side as
clearly as you might. As your loving son, I'll do my best to
"enlighten" you and to defend my own choices as well.

You are right, of course, when you point out the dangers of
secular colleges and universities for Christian young people. I
watched too many of my classmates change from committed
Christians to confirmed agnostics during college to pretend
that both the academic content and the general lifestyle of such
schools are not potentially devastating. As you well know, I
almost fell apart at a secular college myself.

But you make it seem as though the major reason Christian
students give up their faith has to do with their fear of being
scoffed at or dismissed as unsophisticated by the evil hordes of
secular humanists waiting to devour the Children of God. I
think there definitely are professors out there who love to
"deprogram" Christians, but I also think that there is usually a
lot more at stake in the battle for the mind than academic cool-
ness or acceptance. Every student who encounters radical
doubts as a result of his or her academic pursuits is not impressionable or naïve, Dad, and I think you know that. An intelligent person armed with a developing critical perspective
cannot help but encounter very real problems with main-
stream Christianity, no matter how strong their relationship
with God may be. Unless, of course, they refuse to examine
anything that is not already pre-interpreted into the Christian
tradition and deemed safe to consider.

When I was at Haverford, and especially when I was at
Brown, I had to face not only the great Christian thinkers of

history, but the great secular thinkers as well. What is more, my professors were not predisposed to magnify the strengths of the former or the weaknesses of the latter in order to maintain the delicate workings of a particular theological system. They had their biases to be sure—some were even Christians—but as scholars, they sought to focus on the merits of the idea in question, instead of on making sure that it would fit into some specific world-view. You say that was a danger, and I must agree with you.

Regardless of what some people believe, everyone who is not a Christian is not an utter fool. Evolution is not absurd. The Bible is not without ambiguity, and its origins are not above being seriously questioned. Everything in other religions is not godless fabrication and foolishness, and Christians have no corner on faith or sincerity or love. People who are pro-choice are not evil, and abortion is not a simple issue with a simple answer.

The secular world is not all wrong, Dad. That is what your book *Partly Right* is all about. In college, I had to face an array of new ideas, some of which were very compelling. Instead of accepting somebody else's entire system, I had to judge things on their own merits and decide for myself what was true. I had to work out my own salvation with fear and trembling because there was no one there to work it out for me. It was scary sometimes. While there was tremendous risk in that process, there was also tremendous potential for growth.

You told that student of yours who said, "I don't know how my parents could have drilled all that crap into my head," that it might have been because her parents wanted her to know the truth. But how did you know what her parents had taught her in the name of Christianity?

I shudder when I think of some of the things I picked up from other people in my early days as a Christian. I heard prejudices and preferences that were turned into doctrines and interpretations of Scripture that justified sin instead of inspiring repentance. I was once told that everything that happened was God's will—just before I went to Haiti and saw little twelve-year-old girls being sold into prostitution to feed their starving brothers and sisters. I often heard it said that God prospered the people who loved him—even though I know many rich sinners and have seen beautiful, obedient Christians dying in poverty.

Now that stuff really is crap, Dad, but to me it was Christianity, too, until I learned different. Maybe at Eastern, someone would have set me straight, but at some other Christian colleges, maybe not. There was no question, though, that in the glare of secular academia such "truths" could not conceal their falsehood. College is dangerous to be sure. It forced me to question everything I had blindly accepted up until then, but what was ultimately rejected was not the Truth at all. And the faith that emerged in me was strong, because I had done what Paul says to do in 1 Thessalonians 5:19–21, "Do not put out the Spirit's fire; do not treat prophecies with contempt. Test everything. Hold on to the good."

The difference between almost losing my faith at Haverford and thriving as a Christian at Brown wasn't that I stopped testing everything. The difference was that at Brown I kept the Spirit's fire burning in my life. Your letter talked about the fellowship at Brown in glowing terms, and there was a lot happening there, but to tell you the truth, Dad, I wasn't as involved with those groups as you thought I was. They are great for some people, but they were a little too rigid in their beliefs for me.

As I have said, I was not taking anything for granted in college, so I was not very comfortable with people whom I perceived as having made up their minds before they knew all the facts. Still, I didn't need to agree with them about everything to appreciate their sincere faith and excitement, so I went to their meetings once in a while to share the joy of praising God together.

What really kept me going at Brown, though, was my friendship with Jerry White. How we got to be friends is a long story involving a girl whom both of us liked and neither of us wound up with in the end, but what emerged from our rivalry was a strong bond. Like me, Jerry was encountering the doubts and confusion that often go along with sincere thinking, but he didn't seem to be in danger of slipping away from God. We would talk for hours, or study and debate all day long, but he always made sure that we did it from inside our faith. Uncertain as we sometimes were, he made sure we read our Bibles (as listeners—not as students), went to church, and even shared our faith. He got me to pray with him, too, more than I have ever prayed before or since, and as we prayed, God became wonderfully present even in my doubts. We encountered ideas that shook us to our foundations and changed the way we thought about everything. But together we worked out a faith that made sense to us. Deep down I think God put Jerry at Brown just for me, because more than anyone else, he kept my thinking from putting out the Spirit's fire. When college was over, by the grace of God, I had held onto the good.

I did not think enough about how I was going to face the dangers of attending a secular college, which is why it almost did me in. As you said in your letter, there was a lot more going on there than what happened in the classroom and the library, and I didn't handle any of it very well at first.

The lifestyle of a college student is selfish by its very nature. You eat, sleep, read, work, go to class, and do everything else on your own schedule, concerned only with your own grades and your own welfare. At a secular school, that selfishness can very quickly turn into decadence as well. The academic demands at Haverford and Brown were intense, but somehow that didn't keep students from doing a lot of drinking and a lot of sleeping around. People seldom dated steadily, but there were a lot of one-night stands. Drugs and alcohol were abused with impunity. In fact, there was a generally permissive attitude toward anything that did not adversely affect your GPA.

Anytime you find yourself in an atmosphere without limits there is great potential for trouble. Frankly, the lifestyle issues of college were much more dangerous to me than anything I encountered in my classes because, cut off from all the factors that had kept me on the straight and narrow through high school, I found that I had far less discipline than I had given myself credit for. Without my support group to check up on me, or parents to know where I was spending the night, or even a long-time reputation and Christian witness to uphold, I had only my will to rely on for the first time in my life. As you might imagine, my will wasn't up to snuff after so little use, and I quickly found myself doing things I knew were not God's will for me.

That kind of moral crisis, of course, had a tremendous effect on the intellectual issues I was facing at the same time. It is a lot easier to find fault with a faith you are no longer living out, and it is a lot harder to believe in a God you are no longer obeying. College students often make the mistake of thinking that they can separate what they do from what they think and believe, but that sort of mind/body dichotomy is an intellectual myth. Physical sin affects what you think, and mental sin affects how you feel because the two sides of our lives are inexorably tied up together. It is no accident that when people begin to do what they know is wrong, they often begin to be unsure of what they know. That is what happened to me, I'm afraid, and that is why working at Glenn Welch's church saved me. Getting involved in ministry again forced me to clean up my act.

Having conceded that attending a secular college can be a great risk for a committed Christian, let me make one thing perfectly clear: It was a lot safer for me than attending a Christian college.

I was still a fairly new believer when, as a senior in high school, you sent me to visit schools. The thing I most remember was my amazement at how taken for granted Christianity was on those Christian college campuses. Here I was, filled to overflowing with dreams and plans and questions and stories amidst hundreds of kids who had seen it all and heard it all a million times before. It wasn't just that most of them were intellectually uninspired or shallow—beyond that, they were bored with what mattered more than anything in the world to me.

The guys had the same girlie posters hanging in their rooms as at the secular schools, but they bothered me more. People slept through chapel, and it seemed to me it would have been better not to have required chapel at all. The dormitory Bible studies I sat in on were dead. The kids' spiritual lives seemed dead. The whole atmosphere was dead.

Now I was surely one hyper-judgmental high-school kid at the time, Dad, and I don't claim to have gotten the whole picture, but what I did see frightened me. In my secular high school, I had taken a stand for Jesus and was in no danger of taking him for granted. These Christian colleges, however, seemed to have the potential to do something even worse than attacking my faith—they could make it seem boring. No, I thought, I'll take my chances in the real world, where I can talk about my faith out in the open, to believers and non-believers alike, without the fear of boring somebody who has been jaded by overexposure to the joy of it all.

Besides, it also bothered me that those Christian colleges had what you call a Christian world-view. A world-view is something that I believe an individual is supposed to develop in the context of his or her relationship with God, rather than simply accept from an institution. I wanted a school that would teach me how to read and write and think critically, not one that would impart to me a pre-packaged set of ideas and interpretations. Maybe this isn't what Christian colleges do, but it certainly seemed that way to me. I know that most Christian schools may not consciously attempt to indoctrinate their students with a particular system of thought, but all those institutional statements of faith worried me nevertheless. At a secular school I knew there would be a variety of perspectives, and I felt a whole lot safer in the middle of an argument than in the middle of what I perceived be a conspiracy. I may have been grossly unfair—but I think I was also partly right.

My final consideration was purely elitist. I wanted to go to a top school with top professors and top students, and my perception was, and is, that to do that I had to go to a secular school. For whatever reasons, even the best Christian colleges do not carry with them the prestige or the traditions of academic excellence that the upper echelon of secular private colleges have. I was committed to developing my mind to its fullest potential, and no Christian school I visited seemed as singularly committed to intellectual achievement as the finest secular schools.

For all of the trials and tribulations of my college experience, I'm still convinced of this much: I did well to go the route of the secular college. I could have done better, of course, but God was gracious to me, and in the end I think I chose the better path for myself. I won't lie to you, Dad, and tell you that what was right for me is right for every kid. The truth is that every year I send high-school seniors to places like Eastern and Calvin and Seattle Pacific College because I recognize the advantages you outlined in your letter. We may disagree about my case specifically, but we are in full agreement on the most important thing about choosing a college. The ultimate criteria must always be whether a particular school is going to inspire the student to reach his or her fullest potential as a servant of the Kingdom of God.

Love,

Bart

P.S. I was hurt and very angry the night you asked me if I was a homosexual. I thought that you should have known better. I felt as though somehow I had been attacked. At the least, I felt unfairly challenged. But a few hours later, I realized what you had been trying to do.

It is a painful thing to be gay in this world, especially if you are a Christian. There is little understanding and even less compassion. If I were gay, it would have been very hard for me to tell you and Mom about it and risk your rejection. I would have felt isolated, alone with my secret, but probably I would have kept it to myself for fear of losing your acceptance.

But just before you asked me about being a homosexual, both you and Mom let me know that regardless of how I answered, your love for me would not change. You wanted to know, not judge me, and only so you could understand what I was going through. You wanted to be sure that I was not left alone.

As it happens, I am not gay. But it always meant a lot to me to know that I could have been without losing you. God help the child who does not know that.

SEVEN

FLYING LIKE AN EAGLE WHEN YOU FEEL LIKE A TURKEY

Dear Dad,

I think you're going to like this letter. At least I hope you do, because it's about the one thing that I think you were the very best at when I was growing up. I know that you don't consider yourself the perfect father, and as much as I would like to disagree with you, I'm afraid that you're probably right about that (which is why it's so difficult for me to understand how, in spite of yourself, you managed to produce a perfect son!). Whatever else you may have failed to do, Dad, you succeeded in making me believe without a doubt that I was the most essentially wonderful person you had ever laid your eyes on and that anyone who failed to recognize my inestimable value was simply oblivious to the obvious. You made me absolutely sure of myself. And that, more than anything else, has made all the difference in my life.

I know that some people think parenthood is all about instilling the proper principles, developing discipline, and setting a good example, but when everything is said and done, I think it has more to do with creating an indestructible sense of personal significance in a child who is going to need it for the rest of his life.

The more I become involved with ministry, the more I see that the world is a dangerous and hurtful place, filled with broken people who have been overcome and victimized because they lack an understanding of their own value. Regardless of background, everybody experiences failures and disappointments from time to time, and it is hard not to be discouraged or to despair. How people see themselves has a lot to do with how they approach those troubles and whether or not they are able to deal with them. How people see themselves has a lot to do with the other people around them, especially as they are growing up.

You are the first person who taught me that back when I was a little kid sitting in on your sociology lectures at the University of Pennsylvania. I was only nine years old at the time, but I can still remember you explaining Charles Cooley's theory of the Looking Glass Self to the class and how proud I was that I could understand it. It's a pretty simple concept. The basic idea is that how a person sees himself is largely determined by how he thinks the most important people in his world see him. These people are what Cooley calls "significant others."

I didn't realize it then, but as I sat in that classroom, I was already looking at my most significant other. What I saw in your eyes was that I was unbelievably precious to you. A lot has happened between then and now, of course, but I have relied over and over again on that sense of personal significance which both you and Mom gave to me. I never needed it—or both of you—more than when I first moved to Minneapolis to be a youth pastor.

I have already said that the most crucial task for parents is making kids feel that they are infinitely valuable. We are beloved children of God. He sent his own son to redeem us. As Paul puts it, each of us was "bought at a price," and since that price was the life of Jesus himself, we should have no doubt of our worth on any standard. That doesn't mean that we should have delusions of grandeur, though, or think that we are more than we are. "If anyone thinks he is something when he is nothing, he deceives himself" (Galatians 6:3). The flip side to our infinite value is the recognition that we are people with serious limitations.

When I came out of college, I'm afraid I was a long way from that sort of recognition, perhaps because I hadn't yet come up against anything I wanted to do that I couldn't get done. I hate to say that I was arrogant, but I was at the very least a cocky guy who thought he had the world by the tail. I had an Ivy League education, a pretty girlfriend, an exciting new job at a prestigious inner-city church, and, I soon found out, a lot to learn.

It didn't take long for my lessons to begin. Almost from the moment I arrived at Park Avenue, I was in trouble. At first, it seemed as though most of it came from things I couldn't control. The pastor in charge of the youth ministry had teamed me up with another guy on the staff, but just as we began to click as partners, the two of them became involved in a major disagreement that caused all sorts of division within the church and among the street kids we were working with. All of a sudden, my supervisor and my new buddy were completely at odds with one another. Before I knew what I was doing, I threw myself into the middle and began trying to mediate between the two. In my youthful arrogance, I was sure that I could solve everybody's problems in short order.

In fact, all I accomplished for my effort was to undermine both my boss' and my co-worker's confidence and trust in me—even though I wasn't part of the original disagreement. All my efforts failed to make things better, and some actually made things worse. In the end, my co-worker left the church, but not before both he and my boss had been through a spiritual and emotional wringer. I don't think I really understood why Satan is called the author of confusion until I experienced the pain and futility of that struggle, which yielded nothing good at all.

Those problems left me feeling very much alone in a new city, where it seemed like everyone I knew was mad at me. I had tried to help, but I only made things worse for everyone—and I didn't even have a shoulder to cry on. I remember calling home to ask for advice and finding that I couldn't even explain what was happening to me because you and Mom didn't know the people involved. I must have sounded pretty paranoid, I suppose, because what you told me was to stop complaining and concentrate on the ministry instead.

Unfortunately, my ministry wasn't going any better. I had always excelled as a camp counselor and youth speaker, so I assumed that I would be a great youth pastor. The kids at Park

Avenue liked me, and I liked them. I figured I was home free. I quickly realized, however, that there is more to youth ministry than entertaining a bunch of high-school kids. The more aware I became of what I was supposed to be doing, the more I saw that I was failing. The kids in our neighborhood needed more than a Peter Pan-type of youth worker who could get them to think that being a Christian was cool—they needed someone who could patiently guide them beyond emotional conversions into solid relationships with God based on the example of Jesus Christ. They needed a pastor, and, to my dismay, I quickly learned that pastoring is not something I do very well.

I thank God that he provided two real youth pastors—John Hall and Brent Bromstrup—who were willing to guide, encourage, and teach me during our weekly lunches together. Without those faithful brothers, I don't think I would have accomplished anything at all. The rest of the staff at the church gave me a lot of support, too. Despite all their help, I felt like a hippopotamus trying to tap dance. Somehow, God did his own thing in spite of my inadequacies. I saw kids come to know God, and I saw kids grow, but I never stopped feeling like I was a failure at my job, which was especially hard for me because I had never known anything but success until then. I went from being on top of the world to being alone and ineffective in a matter of months. To make matters worse, my girlfriend called to let me know she wasn't my girlfriend anymore. I had been dumped.

I don't know if it sounds as bad to you as it was for me, but for a long time I wondered how I could go on. Even God seemed far away then, and I felt I had completely lost my bearings and was lost at sea. Maybe it seems strange that a youth pastor who was joyously preaching salvation and the love of God was teetering on the edge of despair, but there I was. A light wind would have knocked me over. Then, you and Mom and Lisa showed up.

That family visit to Minneapolis was one of the best weeks of my life. I don't know if any of you knew the way I had begun to think about myself; you couldn't have done anything better if you had. You met everybody, of course, and you heard me out as we toured the city. It did me a world of good just to unburden myself with people who I knew cared about me, to know that my problems were your problems, too.

Even more importantly, you treated me as though I was the same successful person I had been when I left home, instead of like the complete failure I felt like just then. I remember your saying, "We are proud of you," more often than usual, and assuring me that if I couldn't make a go of it there, I could come home and work for you, Dad, because you always needed a person like me.

Lisa, ever the lawyer, took my side and made everybody else out to be a villain, even though my situation was nobody's fault but my own. "You're part of the natural aristocracy, kid, the elite," she told me, knowing I needed to hear it even if it wasn't true. "These people don't appreciate your unique greatness."

Most important of all was Mom, who thought it all through and, right before you left, gave me a pep talk that I'll never forget.

"Bart," she said, "you don't have to just stay here and feel helpless and defeated. You are a smart young man and a loving young man. But right now you have stopped looking at the people around you as people to be creatively loved, and you have started to see them only as part of a situation that is hurting you. You've become selfish. That isn't like you. You can certainly come home if you need to, but before you do, I think you need to see what God has brought you here to learn, and who he has brought you here to love and care for. Maybe you won't be a big star to everybody else, after all. But Dad and I believe in you, and we think you can make it here if you remember who you are."

That visit changed everything for me. The situations did not resolve themselves overnight, of course. When you left, I faced the same problems with the same deficiencies I had before (and still have). My attitude, though, was transformed because I knew that even though I might fail sometimes, I still was infinitely valuable. Even though I couldn't solve everything, I had the ability to make a difference wherever I happened to be. Together, you reminded me of my indestructible sense of personal significance.

That was a turning point in my life. I grew up a lot at Park Avenue, and the people there were patient with me through it all. That pastor, Art Erickson, became a close and valued friend, and God worked mightily in the lives of young people even though I wasn't the most gifted youth worker in the world. Best of all, it was at Park Avenue that I met Marty Thorpe, who is now my altogether wonderful wife. In retrospect, none of that would have happened if I had not had the sense of personal significance that our family helped me to find again—I had it to begin with because you had given it to me. I know that I am infinitely precious because for as long as I can remember I have been infinitely precious to you.

You see, Dad, the things that mattered the most to me when I was a boy, and that still matter the most today, were those times when you let me know that I was your highest priority in the world. Over and over again, you said things and did things that made me sure that I was more important to you than your work, your money, your possessions, your adult friends, and even yourself. (I've thought about it, and the only ones I didn't feel more important than were Mom and Lisa. But Mom and you seemed like one entity, so that didn't really count, and you somehow made Lisa seem like someone you and I should love together, instead of like someone I was competing with.)

I doubt you even remember most of the episodes that made the biggest impressions on me, because they were not the "big events" of my childhood. Rather it was little off-hand comments and casual decisions that let me know who I was and where I stood. Like when we were driving to a church where you were going to preach before we went on to see an afternoon automobile race, and you told me that you would rather go with me than any of your grown-up friends because I was more fun to be with. You probably do not recall exactly what happened that Sunday. I do. It was the Langhorne 150, and Bobby Unser won in the Bardahl Special after Mario Andretti's STP Racer had a flat tire with twenty laps to go. I don't know very much about any of the countless other races we saw together when I was a kid, but that whole day was magical to me after you said that, and I remember every detail.

Later on, when I was seventeen and a new driver, I smashed up cars as though I were racing in the Langhorne 150 myself. Practically every time I drove, I managed to hit something. I had five accidents in three months before you realized that you had to take my license away because I was such a danger to myself and everyone else. Even so, you never said a word about the cars themselves except, "Cars can be replaced—you can't." I paid you back for the repairs as I remember, but that wasn't the point. The point was that I mattered to you more than those cars. The last accident was a bad one, so frightening to me that I barely spoke afterward. When I came home, I was embarrassed and dazed. You took me out to shoot baskets that afternoon. I got the message. So what if I couldn't drive—I was still okay with you.

I know you probably remember the important milestones, like family vacations and my first date and both my graduations, but what I remember is that once you flew back from Chicago and drove straight to the field to be at one of my high-school soccer games and then flew right back again to finish your job in Chicago. You missed a night's sleep because you knew how much your being at that game mattered to me. I remember that stuff because it is what convinced me that, no matter what happened, I definitely counted for something.

Sometimes it's hard for a kid to believe that he counts, you know. A lot of bad things happen. Being beaten up at school can really destroy a kid's self-esteem and rob him of any sense of joy. I know that because when I was in sixth grade, I was beaten up on an almost daily basis. It was as much a part of my school day as lunch, and there was nothing I could do about it except wait until I either got bigger or we moved to another state. I was a little kid with a big mouth—a fatal combination in junior high. In elementary school the biggest kid in the class, Daniel Keough, had been my friend and protected me from harm, but Daniel ended up assigned to a different building altogether in junior high, and from then on I was a walking target. Even when the other guys got tired of pounding me, it didn't stop—the girls beat me up.

I can laugh about it now, but that was a terrible year for me. I hated going to school, and I walked the halls in fear of the numerous bullies who took turns making my life miserable. I know I told you about some of the beatings I took, Dad, but I couldn't tell you about all of them because I was so embarrassed. It was humiliating to be so vulnerable, and I especially did not want you to know about it because of the stories you had told me about your own childhood. You never got beat up unless there was more than one guy, and even then, you made them pay for it. You were tough. I was scared and ashamed of it.

One day, my teacher called me out of class and sent me to the principal's office. I hadn't done anything wrong, but I was worried anyway—you always worry when they call you to the principal's office. When I got there, though, you were standing at the desk signing me out of school for a "family emergency." Some emergency—you took me out to eat lunch in a deli and then we went to an afternoon movie, which I liked so much that we sat through the second show. "School," you said, "is never as important as you are."

The reason those things made such a deep impression on me was because I knew you had chosen me over other things. Whenever you demonstrated your priorities, where things stood relative to one another in your life, I found that I was way up at the top. You had other things to worry about, of course, but none of them mattered more than I did. I have my own set of priorities now, and it's not the same as yours except right at the top. There, where the most important things in life are arranged, you and I are remarkably similar. If I ever have a son, I want him to have experiences like I did, where he cannot miss the realization that, at least to his father, he is infinitely more valuable than anything in the world.

There is something else that you gave me that I want to give to my son, so when the world defeats him he will not be destroyed. Along with the knowledge that he is infinitely valuable, I want him to realize that he can make a difference in his world, no matter what the situation may be.

In the end, it is undoubtedly the belief that our actions and decisions matter and can change things that gives our lives meaning and purpose. Armed with that belief, people can face the most overwhelming situation with hope, knowing that, win or lose, they have the potential to act instead of simply being acted upon. Without it, even people in the midst of great blessings cannot feel secure because they are always at the mercy of the people and circumstances that surround them. Unless we believe we can affect the world, we are bound to become its victims.

When I first met Marty, she was a counselor for chemically dependent women, most of whom were also poor. Every woman's story was different in some ways, but there was always one common feature; these women had all stopped believing that they controlled their own lives. People who give up that belief are bound to become somebody's victims. They can only react to the world and never act on it themselves.

I didn't start out believing I could make a difference, of course. No one does. We are born utterly dependent, unable to do anything at all for ourselves—except make a mess (which we do quite well). Gradually I became more independent, but as I grew up, I experienced periodic reminders of my extensive limitations. Like getting lost in a shopping mall . . . running away from home when I was seven and realizing I had nowhere to go . . . getting punished . . . or finding out at the age of eighteen that you did not have to put me through college. You did not even have to feed me anymore. Indeed, growing up with someone as powerful as you for my father, it was easy for me to believe that, far from being capable of changing the world, I wasn't really able to do much of anything important. You, however, could do anything and everything. At least I always thought you could when I was a boy.

You and Mom both went to great lengths to show me that I was wrong, that I could make a difference, and that I could do things that you or Mom or anybody else in the world could never do, because God had made me.

When I was in the second grade, there was a new kid in my class named Larry. Larry was different from the other kids, and everybody disliked him from the moment he arrived. Looking back, I am sure he had a learning disability, but all I knew then was that he talked strangely, dressed badly, and wasn't very good at anything. Even Miss Hutchinson, our teacher, seemed to wish he would go away.

We were learning to read that year, using flash cards, and when it was Larry's turn, he would miss the words so badly that we all thought he was doing it on purpose. Try as she might, nothing Miss Hutchinson did could make him understand. Day after day, I watched him miss as the class laughed at his efforts.

It was even worse for Larry on the playground. We excluded him from our games with the special cruelty of youth. Once in a while, somebody picked a fight with him just so the rest of us could make fun of his wild lunges and strange noises. It bothered me to see him so mistreated, but because my own position among the other kids was fairly insecure, I held my tongue.

It went on like that until, one day, Miss Hutchinson lost her patience. As Larry missed yet another word, and the class dissolved into giggles, he tried to cover his embarrassment by joining in the laughter. Suddenly, Miss Hutchinson rushed up to him, grabbed him by the hair and pulled his head back so he was looking straight up, with his mouth wide open. "Stop it!" she hissed, as the classroom fell silent, "Stop it right now! Now you . . . sit down!" She released him, and he slouched into his seat. The class was back to normal before too long, but I wasn't.

By the time I got home, I was so upset, I blurted out the whole story to you and Mom the moment I came through the door. I don't know what I expected you to do, but it certainly wasn't what you did. You told me that you couldn't say anything to Miss Hutchinson because you had not been there, but that if I wanted to talk to her, you would come and be there with me.

Sure enough, the next morning we went to school early, and I went in to face her while you stood in the doorway, watching and making me brave. I told her how upset I was and how bad I felt about what she had done to Larry, and when I was done, she took a deep breath. I was right, she said, and she was sorry for losing her temper. She promised me that she would apologize to Larry, and then we even talked about ways we could both try to be kinder to him. She even thanked me for caring enough to come and talk to her.

That was the first time I believed I could make a difference, and it gave me a strange sensation of power. Miss Hutchinson was kinder to Larry, and so was I. We became friends that year.

Although Larry was never the most popular boy in the second grade, he ceased to be an outcast, and he did have some happy moments. Later on, he came to my birthday party, and I think it was the only one he was invited to all year. Lisa always orchestrated my parties with great style, and that year she rigged it so Larry even won some of the games. There is a photograph of that party, and in it there is one little face smiling a strange, wild smile.

I wonder what became of Larry after that year. Miss Hutchinson became my favorite teacher of all time. After all, she was part of the most important lesson I ever learned: Bart Campolo was not only valuable, he also had the capability to be an effective force for good in the world.

Mom took me along to visit her elderly friends in order to teach me the same thing. I didn't like those visits at first, but she insisted that I go with her anyway and always told me how much my being there meant to the old women we visited. It was boring, usually, sitting around talking and being polite, but once I saw that she was right, that those visits were bright spots in those people's routinized lives, trying to charm them became the best kind of child's game for me. Once again, I felt powerful. There was something important I could do that simply would not be done if I did not do it, and I liked that. I still do.

Knowing I could make a difference for other people helped me to believe I could change my own circumstances, too. Years after my experience with Larry and Miss Hutchinson, I came up against a basketball coach from the old school of motivation-through-fear. You know, Dad, it seems unfair that I inherited your baldness, but missed out on your thick skin. Before long, Coach Jackson's style had turned this sensitive little kid into an emotional wreck.

I did my best to take it like a man (whatever that means), but I always came home gloomy and depressed. I felt victimized by his constant threats and insults, but helpless to do anything about it. It is one thing to take a stand for someone else, but another thing completely to face up to your own tormentor. Finally, though, Coach Jackson went too far.

In the middle of a big game, he pulled me out for making a mental error. In front of the entire team, my mother, and my grandmother, he swore at me and told me that my head was in a location where, anatomically speaking, I knew it could not have been. I was utterly humiliated and by the time the game was over all I wanted was to quit the team and be done with it.

You, ever sensitive to my emotional discomfort, forbade it. I could only quit, you said, *after* I confronted Coach Jackson with my objections to his treatment of me. Since such a move was clearly suicidal, I figured that you had simply grown bored with fatherhood and were looking for a way out—and I noted that this time you didn't offer to go along with me. But I went anyway.

Coach Jackson wasn't quite as compassionate as Miss Hutchinson had been, but he understood enough of what I said to promise to lay off. "I was only trying to get you to play your best," he said, and I am sure that that was true. In any case, things got better.

Even if he hadn't listened to me, just saying what I did transformed the entire situation for me. I was no longer a helpless victim in my own mind. I learned that I could act. People do not always treat me the way I would like to be treated, but the things you taught me to believe about myself let me recognize that I do not deserve to be treated badly, and I do not have to accept it.

I see so many people here in the city, especially women, who are abused and victimized because they have forgotten or have never known their infinite value and their capability to make a difference in their own lives and in the lives of other people. They are susceptible to evil in whatever form it approaches them because they see themselves as people who deserve to be abused and who are unable to do anything to escape that abuse when it comes.

I once asked a friend of mine, a former prostitute, how she began, how she came to be exploited by strangers. What I found out was that she had been so sexually abused as a child that she had lost any sense of her own value. Made to believe she deserved to be hurt, she found herself in one bad relationship after another until finally a man approached her who told her she was pretty and that he loved her and wanted to take care of her. "I was so messed up, and he took me in. He was the first person who ever really loved me." She believed in that man, too, even though he was a pimp who sent her out to earn him money each night with her body. He told her that she was his girl, and she believed him because she didn't know any better.

There's one more thing to be said about the indestructible sense of personal significance that you gave to me: it made it a whole lot easier for me to become a Christian.

It's so hard for some people to believe that they were created to be part of the Kingdom of God because they feel worthless by worldly standards. Yet God did create them, and that fact alone endows them with the worth that comes from being the handiwork of the Almighty.

For others, it is unthinkable that someone would love them so much that he would sacrifice his own life to save theirs, because no one has ever placed them anywhere so high on a list of priorities. John 3:16 notwithstanding, they don't realize that Jesus' love for each of us is relentless and pure and that we're so precious to him that he died to take away the sins that otherwise would have separated us from him forever.

Even many who believe in the love of God find it unbelievable that they can make a decision to accept that love and become a new creation in the process. Yet that is exactly what God calls us to do; that is what his power working in our lives allows us to do if we let it. We not only become his children but also his servants, through whom he can change the lives of others, and the world itself.

For me, though, all that stuff was easy. The Gospel was the natural extension of a love I had experienced all my life. It was the ultimate, infinite expression of realities that had been expressed to me for as long as I could remember: I had value—I was worth making sacrifices for—and I could make decisions that could change my life and the lives of other people.

Since I became a Christian, there have been all sorts of doubts and difficulties, and I have often found the peripheral issues of the faith hard to reconcile. At the center of it all, though, is the Good News of the love of God in the person of Jesus Christ, and the call to be transformed into a new creation. That was and is easy for me to understand and embrace.

Thanks Dad.

Love,

Bart

*   *   *   *

Dear Bart,

Your letter makes me think that I did something right in raising you. Making a kid believe in himself is one of the most important things that a father can do for his son. This is especially true during those years when a boy's father is his "significant other." During those years, what a boy thinks of himself is dependent upon what he thinks his father thinks of him.

Making you feel good about yourself was a more difficult task than you suspect. I wanted to build up your self-confidence without making you cocky—and with teenagers there is a very fine line between the two. Like most kids in their teens, you seemed to fluctuate between thinking too highly of yourself and being down on yourself. Let me remind you of a series of events that brilliantly illustrates what I mean.

You had it all going for you in your senior year in high school. You were a star soccer player, and, after taking your SAT tests, you were declared a National Merit Scholar. There was a special scholarship available at a very prestigious college for students who had this combination of abilities. You and I were both convinced that you were going to win that scholarship. There was only one thing standing between you and what would have amounted to a free education, and that was an interview with the awards committee. Your ease with people and your gift of gab made both of us overconfident, and I believe your over confidence was your downfall. It was hard for both of us when the committee passed over you. So far as I could figure, you lost out because the committee thought you were a little too sure of yourself and maybe even a bit arrogant.

When you got the news of being rejected, you went into a depression that was nothing less than horrible. Mom and I really got worried about you. You had lost something. The old Bart seemed to be gone, and the new one was shaky. Your depression was taking a spiritual toll on you, too. I had the sense that you felt that God was a million miles away from you.

For the next few months, you seemed to be going nowhere fast. The early summer following your graduation from high school was particularly painful. You were joyless and seemed devoid of any kind of ambition. A good job was nowhere to be found, and being unemployed only added to your sense of woe. I knew that I had to do something to help restore you to that properly balanced kid who once had had it all together. It was time for me to consider some viable options.

Toward the end of June, I called some of my friends who had connections. I figured that if you had a good job and earned some decent money, you might be able to climb out of the doldrums. Partly through my efforts, you got a job at a warehouse for a camera company. Things, however, didn't get much better for you. Because of your careless driving and numerous accidents, we felt we could no longer maintain car insurance for you, and that meant you had a twenty-mile round trip to and from work each day on your bike. You really had a tough time of it and came home incredibly depressed, especially on rainy days.

I wasn't surprised that you had the kind of driving record that had gotten you into this mess. Sometimes when a person is down on himself, he will unconsciously self-destruct. There are enough psychological studies to verify this claim for anyone who doubts it. Someone in a deeply negative state of mind can even be subconsciously suicidal in ways that contribute to his being accident-prone.

When summer ended and you started in at Haverford College, I thought things would get better, but they didn't. You returned to school early to go out for the soccer team, but a reaction to a bee sting plus a sprained knee put you out of commission and kept your collegiate sports career from ever getting off the ground. You were severely affected—much more than I think you realize. Mom and I walked the floors at night wondering and talking about how we could get you out of it. Most of all, we prayed.

A breakthrough came when a pastor friend of mine, Glenn Welch, contacted me and told me that he needed someone to help him with the youth work at his church. I immediately thought of you. I not only knew that you could do the job, but I saw the position as an opportunity for you to regain your self-confidence.

At first, I thought that you might not accept the position. You hemmed and hawed when we discussed the matter. Your best excuse was that you didn't have a car, and a car would be needed if you were to work as a youth minister in a suburban church. I offered you my car. I was so desperate to see you take this position that I would have done anything in my power to make it attractive to you. In the end, I didn't have to do too much. You got together the money to buy an ancient Dodge, and you were on your way.

From the first week you worked at Christ United Methodist Church, things picked up. Kids who hadn't been attending youth meetings for months started turning out because you made church fun for them. Glenn told me that your enthusiasm was contagious, and in just a few weeks, you had the youth program in high gear. Teenagers were coming to know Christ in a new and personal way. Parents were raving about the time and interest you spent on their kids. I was pleased with the reports, but what really thrilled me was the change in your attitude and demeanor. Success in youth work had gotten your juices going again, and your self-confidence was more than restored. You were on a roll again.

There is no doubt that getting you into a situation where you could do something you could be proud of and that others would praise had more to do with building you up than anything I could have said or done for you directly. If you thank me for believing in you, I can only say that it was easy to believe in you. You had more abilities than I ever dreamed of having at your age. It was only a matter of getting you into a context where you could do your thing without being under pressure. Glenn Welch and that wonderful church of his gave you that chance, and Mom and I will always be grateful to them for that.

The fact that I was able to influence your sense of self-worth so heavily was due to your love for me. You had made me into what we sociologists would call your "significant other." In other words, you had made me into that person who was so important to you that what you thought of yourself was highly determined by what you thought I thought of you. You honored me and trusted me by doing that. I do not know for sure how I was able to get you to do this, or even if I was primarily responsible for engineering your feelings, but I was well aware that you looked up to me and that I could easily have created destructive disillusionment had I behaved in a way that disgraced you or hurt you. As a father, I tried to be guided by the words of an old, old hymn that I learned when I was a boy:

I would be true, for there are those who trust me.
I would be pure, for there are those who care.
I would be strong, for there is much to suffer.
I would be brave, for there is much to dare.

Recently, a man I had once counseled told me that he was planning to walk out on his wife and children. I asked him if he had fully considered what his leaving would do to his boy, whom I knew idolized him. The man returned my question with a question of his own and asked, "You don't expect me to sacrifice my happiness for my wife and kids, do you?"

"Of course I do," I answered. "I really can't think of anyone more worthy of such a sacrifice."

He left his wife and children in spite of my probing question, and four years later, his son was arrested in a drug bust. There is a great likelihood that the son's problems were related to his father's leaving the family to live with another woman. The one from whom that son had obtained his sense of worth had betrayed the boy's trust. Small wonder that the

Scriptures say that the sins of the fathers shall be visited upon the children (Exodus 20:5–6).

I wonder if fathers who consider divorces have any idea of how what they plan to do affects their kids. Children often blame the break-up of their parents' marriage on themselves and feel that if they had been better children, their fathers wouldn't have left. I wonder if fathers have any idea what this kind of thinking can do to kids and how it can destroy their sense of worth and their self-confidence. No simple heart-to-heart talk with a child is likely to dissipate the consequences of desertion. A man had better be absolutely sure that there is no way he can stay with his family before he walks out on them. If his kids end up destroyed because dad has found a new romance, there will be a special judgment for that man. Jesus said:

> But whoso shall offend one of these little ones which believe in me, it were better for him that a millstone were hanged about his neck, and that he were drowned in the depth of the sea.
>
> *Matthew 18:6*

I must say that staying with Mom was not a sacrificial thing. She is the kind of wife who has always made me grateful to be married to her. Nonetheless, the realization that I could easily have messed up your life played no small part in keeping me from disastrous actions. I knew that I could easily destroy that positive image that you had of me and, in so doing, destroy the positive image you had of yourself. Such are the wages of sin.

All of this is to say that if you think of me as a good father, it is in part due to the fact that you were a good son. We helped to create each other.

Love,

Dad

EIGHT

WHAT ARE YOU GOING TO DO WHEN YOU GROW UP?

Dear Bart,

One of my biggest concerns was what you would do about a choice of vocation. From the time you were a little boy, we always discussed what your future plans might be. I remember you coming in from play when you were about six years old, tossing a ball back and forth from one hand to the other. "Remember when we talked about what I was going to be when I grew up?" you asked. "Well, we decided! I'm going to be a juggler. And look! I already know how to do the bottom part!"

I often told you that I wanted you to choose a "Kingdom" vocation. By that, I meant a vocation in which you would do all that you could, given your gifts and privileges, to change the world into the kind of world that God wants it to be. I wanted you to realize that becoming a Christian involves much more than just accepting certain biblical truths and living out a personal morality that is in harmony with the will of God. I wanted you to recognize that, in gratitude for what God in Christ did for us, all of life should be lived in grateful service to him.

> I beseech you therefore, brethren, by the mercies of God, that ye present your bodies a living sacrifice, holy, acceptable unto God, which is your reasonable service. And be not conformed to this world: but be ye transformed by the renewing of your mind, that ye may prove what is that good, and acceptable, and perfect will of God.
>
> *Romans 12:1–2*

149

This commitment requires that in choosing a vocation every person ought to ask, "If Jesus were in my place, with my talents and my opportunities, what would he do with his life?"

It is not so much that I question the choices that some young people make, as it is that I question the reasons they make them. To become a lawyer is not a bad thing. It becomes a bad thing, however, when the primary reason for going into the profession is to make big money. There are too many lawyers who are willing to participate in suits against anyone for any reason as long as the price is right.

Ralph, one of the inner-city missionaries who work with our organization, the Evangelical Association for the Promotion of Education (EAPE), in Philadelphia, was driving some children to a Bible club. In attempting to change lanes on the expressway, he brushed the van against the rear fender of another vehicle. The man whose car he hit told Ralph that the accident was nothing to worry about and that they didn't have to call the police. He asked that Ralph sign a paper admitting guilt and told him that they could settle the matter later. The man said he didn't want to hold up all those kids on the way to their party. Ralph, who had come from a small town in Texas, was accustomed to trusting people. Unaware of the ways of big-city shysters, he signed the paper. An hour or so later, the man picked up some friends and drove to the hospital. All of them claimed to have been "grievously" injured in the accident. The following day each of them filed suit against our missionary organization, putting its future existence in jeopardy.

The lawyer handling the case was quite cynical about the whole thing and said that he figured that our insurance would cover it. Legal actions like this are carried out by all too many lawyers and have been responsible for driving out of existence many of the inner-city programs designed to help socially disadvantaged kids.

Thanks to the good work of the dedicated Christian lawyers on EAPE's Board of Directors, our organization will probably not be harmed by these unfair actions against us. So you see there is not only the potential for using the legal profession to do greater harm but also the opportunity a Christian lawyer has to aid and protect Christian ministry.

I would like to see Christian lawyers join together and get the state bar associations to do something to police their profession and keep things like the suit against EAPE from happening.

They need to commit themselves to changing the legal system for the better.

Most of all, I want to see young people become lawyers because they are committed to justice for the poor. There are plenty of lawyers who are willing to be "hired guns" for the rich, but very few are committed to working for the poor. Most poor people find it too expensive to take advantage of the American legal system. They simply cannot afford the high cost of justice in this country. It would be wonderful if there were large numbers of Christian young people willing to spend their lives standing up for those who have no voice.

From time to time, I meet lawyers who see their vocation in "Kingdom" terms and who, in the process, are willing to forego wealth. This kind of Christian service really turns me on. There is so much good that lawyers like that can do, and there is so much hope that they can bring to those people who feel trampled by the system.

Young people who want to be doctors also should see their calling as a Kingdom vocation. Joining the medical profession is certainly one way to identify with the Jesus who is also called the Great Physician. Unfortunately, not enough pre-med students see their vocation this way. I get more and more depressed as I read about studies that reveal that the most-often-cited reason for applying to medical school is because the applicants see the medical profession as a way to get rich.

Christian young people must be better than that. They should want to become doctors in order to serve hurting people in the name of their Lord. They ought to seek careers in medicine because they want to minister to the sick and the dying. There is a desperate need for Christian doctors who are willing to make a major commitment to the poor, both in the Third World and here in the United States. Our mission organization has clinics in Haiti but no doctor to work in them. We have Christian community centers located in poor neighborhoods in Philadelphia, where we would very much like to provide medical services for neglected people, but we cannot find a doctor who is willing to sacrifice a lucrative income to do the job.

I don't want to paint too bleak a picture of the medical profession. I do know doctors who are taking their Christian discipleship seriously and are providing some wonderful models for young people. For instance, there is a group of doctors in Lancaster, Pennsylvania, who have come up with a unique plan that enables them to serve the people of the Third World. They have set up a clinic in a Central American country and they take turns each year serving there. The income from the medical practice they share in Lancaster is evenly divided among them so that the one in the field receives the same salary as those who keep the home office going.

Another group of Christian doctors and nurses I know in Pittsburgh have also come up with a Kingdom-like way of practicing medicine. They have turned their backs on the possibility for great wealth and set up a clinic in one of the poorest sections of their city. Half of their patients come from the poorest of the poor of the city, and these people are charged solely in accord with their ability to pay. The other half of the patients who come are well-off people who are encouraged by their pastors to patronize the clinic. The income from the paying patients is enough to keep the clinic going and provides the doctors and nurses with more than enough for their own needs.

I'm sure there are a lot of other opportunities for young people to go into medicine that would reflect the radical values of Christ and give evidence that they are committed to Kingdom vocations. I don't want to seem like I'm picking on doctors and lawyers alone, though. I worry about stockbrokers, businessmen, and blue-collar workers for the same reasons. Vocation should never be primarily determined by money or prestige. Vocation should be a means to Christian service.

I never thought that you would choose either the legal or medical profession or get into the nuts and bolts of business, Bart. I always had the feeling that you would choose to do something that had to do with talking. I remember the time when, at the age of seven, you discovered that I got paid for preaching. Mom and I had taken you along to a fund-raising banquet for Young Life, where I had been the featured speaker. On the way home, you overheard us discussing what we were going to do with my honorarium. You broke in and asked incredulously, "Do you mean that they gave you money just for talking?" When I answered yes, I remember you saying, "What a deal! You get paid to talk! That's what I'm going to do when I grow up!" I don't know whether or not that discovery of yours qualifies as a divine calling, but there was no doubt in my mind that you had been smitten by the idea of being a public speaker. Fortunately, you had the talent to make your dream a reality.

You could have used your gifts in a number of ways, and I was genuinely touched when you decided to go into Christian ministry. The fact that you have committed yourself to using your speaking to promote and develop an inner-city mission program really pleases me. Your ability to articulate the hurts of inner-city kids and your skill in recruiting young people to volunteer to work with you are great assets in your efforts to revitalize inner-city churches. I like your idea of getting college kids to give their summers to run day camps and youth programs out of inner-city churches, which so often lack both human and financial resources. Your gifts seem ideally suited to turning collegians on to the possibilities for evangelism among urban youth. I am also confident that as you tell your story in the better-off suburban churches, you will be able to raise the necessary financial support to make these programs go. My prayers go with you. As far as Kingdom Builders Supply goes, I am behind you all the way.

I know that there are a number of people who see you as trying to "follow in your dad's footsteps." No doubt, some of them wonder if I pressured you into your ministry since it is so much like mine. What you are doing is so much in line with what pleases me, that some of my own friends are wondering whether or not I pushed you into this ministry for vicarious gratification.

Personally, I think that living vicariously through one's children has gotten an undeserved bad name. In ancient days, it was a primary motivation for having children. Perhaps you remember learning in Sunday school that the Sadducees of biblical times had no belief in the afterlife. Consequently, they thought that the only life possible after death was through one's children. While we Christians would not go along with that kind of thinking, I believe that kids should recognize that there is something very right about allowing their parents to gain some fulfillment from living vicariously through them. Needless to say, this should not be carried to extremes. We all know stories of parents who have ruined their children's lives by pressuring them into doing things that weren't particularly good for them. There are countless stories of kids who were made to be in kiddie beauty contests, to play sports, or to sing in the church choir solely to satisfy their parents' ego needs with little regard for the kids themselves. When oppressive conditions are eliminated, however, there are all kinds of wonderful, positive strokes that parents can get from having their kids do what they always wished they could have done.

My father was a poor, uneducated Italian immigrant who had little opportunity to do much more than earn a living for his family. When I was in college, he came to see me play in a basketball game in which I was a high scorer and won the game with a clutch basket. My father was not someone who showed his emotions very often, but after the game he hugged me and told me I had made him very happy. It was one of the few times that he ever hugged me, and when he stepped back, I noticed that he had tears in his eyes. I had always liked playing basketball, but I was doubly thrilled that night at having made my dad feel so good. It seemed to me to have been one small way of paying him back for all he had done for me. A funny thing, Bart, is that once you did the same thing for me in a basketball game when you came off the bench for your high school and won the game with a nineteen-point effort. I got more of a thrill out of that game than I did out of any that I had ever played myself. I guess what goes around, comes around. If getting vicarious kicks through your kids' accomplishments is wrong, then judge me guilty.

I know that all of this puts some pressure on you, and hope you don't find it difficult. When it came to your choice of a vocation, I got tremendous gratification when you decided to go into a Christian ministry that is something like my own. At the same time, I hope you made your decision because you believed it was the will of God for you and, therefore, the right thing for you to do with your life. Pleasing your old man might be a nice thing to do, but pleasing your Heavenly Father is what is ultimately important.

As you made your decision, I assume you did a lot of praying, but I don't think that God spoke to you in a loud, clear voice. He has seldom communicated with me in such a dramatic fashion. Unfortunately, there are always people waiting for some kind of crystal-clear message as confirmation from God about what they should do in life. Some of them, like your Grandpop Davidson, get that kind of calling, and their experiences can easily leave the rest of us feeling that we also should have had some kind of direct and unquestionable word from God. Grandpop can tell you exactly how and when the call to Christian ministry came to him. He can describe the church service in which he came to realize that God had called him into the gospel ministry. That wasn't the way it was for me, and as I ask around, I have found that it wasn't the way most people received the call to do whatever it is they are doing for God. Most of us move forward in life with fear and trembling, lacking the absolute certainty that everyone desires.

Some in Christian ministry have told me that they simply always knew what God created them to do. They have explained to me that being in ministry was something they grew up believing was right for them. Yet there are others I know who have prayed diligently for God's leading but still lack any kind of assurance about their calling and struggle over the question almost every day of their lives. Still others (like myself) have come to accept a sense of calling primarily through rational reflection on the question of how their lives might best be used to impact the world with the love and justice of God.

As I worked my way through college, I was constantly taking stock of what it was that I was able to do (college is a good place to test one's self out on such matters) and trying to figure out what sorts of things gave me a sense of personal fulfillment. When it comes to choosing a vocation, I think that having a realistic view of one's abilities is of utmost importance. The problem is not that God can't impart new gifts to equip a person to do things hitherto unthinkable. As a matter of fact, there are many cases, both in the Bible and in everyday life, that validate the fact that if God calls somebody to do something, he will provide whatever is necessary to carry out that calling. The story of Moses is a case in point. Certainly Aaron, his brother, had better gifts for being a spokesman for Israel. Yet it was Moses whom God called, and it was Moses whom he used to tell old Pharaoh to let the children of Israel leave Egypt. Nevertheless, I think that in many cases God endows us by birth and upbringing with the gifts that are needed for us to carry out his will for our lives. In my case, it was after careful consideration of what I could and could not do that I decided to make preaching my vocation.

Personally, I think there are too many people who have taken up the preaching ministry, because of some misled sense of obligation without having given enough consideration to the question as to whether or not they had the ability to preach. Consequently, there are a lot of preachers in the pulpits of America who are not gifted enough to articulate the gospel with the excitement or artistry that it deserves. It is even worse when such preachers fail in the ministry and end up blaming either God or the church people for their own failures, often giving up the ministry, bitter and broken, and sometimes even turning from God.

In the choice of a vocation, I think a person ought to be as objective as possible in assessing what is possible for him or her to do. It is a good thing in this process to enlist the advice of close friends and parents. People who know you well and have had a chance to observe you over the years can provide good insights as to what your gifts and abilities are as well as your shortcomings. Talking to your pastor is a good thing, as is consulting with a professional counselor. These people should not, however, ultimately determine what is decided. Caution must be exercised to taking advice. I know of some good candidates for the ministry who were steered away from church vocations by well-meaning secular high-school counselors who found full-time Christian vocations beyond their comprehension or sphere of expertise. Studying the Minnesota

Multiphasic Personality Test, which is given to most high-school students, can provide some help in assessing your interests and abilities, but such a test should not be considered the ultimate determiner of anyone's choice of vocation.

In your case, you had a particularly valuable forum to help you review your capabilities. You had your circle of close high-school buddies. Those guys you hung out with had come to know Christ about the same time you did, and together you formed a support group to keep each other faithful to his Christian commitment. I know you regularly prayed for them, asking God to give direction to their lives, and I suppose that they did the same for you. In many ways, they knew more about you than I did. I'm curious, Bart, did you get confirmation for your calling from them? Were they honest with you in helping you to evaluate your calling? The Bible says that the prayers of faithful friends accomplish a great deal of good.

There was something else I did as I was going through the struggle of trying to figure out what God wanted me to do with my life. I went on a retreat all by myself. I was nineteen years old and at the end of my sophomore year of college when I took a whole day and dedicated it completely to seeking God's will for my life. I drove to an old YMCA camp near Medford, New Jersey, and spent the day walking, sitting, thinking, and praying. I had often gone to that camp when I was in high school. I had gone there for numerous church retreats and Bible conferences. It was the scene of some happy teenage romances. That camp was capable of conjuring up an endless array of pleasant memories of friends and good times. It was also a place where I had experienced God in special ways. For me that camp was holy ground.

The campgrounds were empty that day in late May when I took my retreat there. I arrived early in the morning and did not leave until late in the afternoon. During those hours alone with God, I tried to let him speak to me. I remained still for a long time and said nothing. I "centered down" as some of my Quaker friends would say. I waited in the stillness for that soft, still voice of God. I waited for some kind of stirring in the depths of my being. Nothing happened. There was no voice and there were no stirrings, but there was something else. A strange peace came over me; a very pleasant calm pervaded my being. I knew that God knew what I was thinking of doing with my life, and I came away from that day with the feeling that God felt that it was okay. I don't know why I don't do that sort of thing more often.

It occurs to me that Jesus took forty days in the wilderness to be alone with his Father before setting out to fulfill his calling. Perhaps if all of us took that kind of time to purify ourselves and seek his face, we, too, might sense the Holy Spirit falling upon us and a voice from heaven saying, "This is my beloved child in whom I am well pleased."

Perhaps the most important thing I can say to you about choosing a vocation is that God leads us one day at a time. Very often students of mine come to me and ask how to discover God's plan for their lives. I always respond by saying to them that they are asking for too much. I'm not sure that God promises anywhere in Scripture to reveal his entire plan for life to anyone. I tell my students that the real question is what God wants them to do right then—what decisions should be made that day.

When I was nineteen, I made a decision to be a pastor. That meant that I should plan to go through college and seminary and that's what I did. Then I pastored churches for a few years. By the time I was thirty, I had a sense that I ought to be doing something else with my life. No small part of that realization was the discovery that pastoring was no longer providing the excitement or fulfillment that it did during my earlier years.

To be honest about it, I wasn't too good at some aspects of being a pastor; I was not as patient or as willing to listen as I should have been. Pastoring is not easy, and I admire and respect those who are able to do it well more than I can tell you. Fortunately, I had been taking some graduate work on my days off and had accumulated enough credit to qualify as a college teacher. Both Eastern College and the University of Pennsylvania gave me invitations to teach. It wasn't long before I left the pastorate for the halls of academia.

When I first started teaching at Penn, my mother was really upset. She thought that I had abandoned my calling to serve God. In reality, the same God who had led me into the pastorate was now leading me into something new to do for him. My years at Penn provided me with a unique opportunity to minister in a secular community, and I know I made a difference in my years there. My background as a pastor enabled me to provide counsel to a lot of troubled, mixed-up kids. My roots in the church made it possible for me to help a good number of collegians to find their way into Christian fellowship. At the same time, my sojourn at Penn forced me to take academic studies very seriously, and I learned things during those years that have helped me immeasurably in what I have been called to say and write for the Christian community.

You know that my decision to leave the University of Pennsylvania was a hard one. Yet after these many years at Eastern College, I know that that decision optimized what I could do for the Kingdom. Because Eastern is a Christian college, I have been encouraged in my endeavors to develop missionary programs. Without Eastern, I doubt if I could have started EAPE and all its outreach programs in urban America and in Third World countries. Eastern has given me office space for EAPE, and the students from the college provide countless hours of sacrificial service in our many missionary projects.

As I look back over the years, I see that each thing I did prepared me for the next. When I went into the pastorate, I did not know that I was being prepared for service in a secular university. Nor did I see that what happened to me at Penn was God's way of preparing me for my present ministry. In short, when I decided on that personal retreat that it was God's will for me to become a pastor, I did *not* come to grips with what God wanted me to do with my whole life—I only accepted what I was to do during the *next stage* of my life.

What I am trying to say to you is that life is never settled. Having made a decision to be in one particular ministry, be sure to be aware that God may have something new for you to do some day. Keep your eyes and mind open, listen to those who love you, take time to retreat to aloneness with God and always be ready for something new from him. His will for you in the years to come may lead you into some presently unimaginable avenues of service. Be ever ready to go adventuring with God.

Love,

Dad

*   *   *   *

Dear Dad,

Your letter about choosing a vocation made me smile because it reminded me of a conversation we had on an airplane when I was in between colleges, somewhere around the age of twenty. I say "in between" because you and Mom never liked the term "dropped out," even though that was probably closer to the truth at the time. Anyway, I was waxing eloquent on the difficulties of choosing a career in the absence of a specific spiritual revelation from on high when you cut me off in mid-soliloquy.

"It's simple," you said bluntly. "You look at the needs of the world that you know about and decide which ones you can relate to or which ones hurt you the most. You figure out what gifts and abilities God has given you to work with and how you can best use them to meet the needs he has laid on your heart. Then you get the training you need and get to work."

Your letter shows that even though you may have become a little more sophisticated over the years, you haven't really changed much.

Of course, that approach only works if the person you are talking to already has the kind of strong sense of personal significance that I wrote to you about in an earlier letter, along with a commitment to serving the Kingdom of God. You did a good job of explaining how a person like that ought to go about finding his or her specific direction, but the real question in my mind is how can parents instill the heart of a servant in their child? In the midst of the most self-indulgent, self-gratifying, self-oriented culture in the history of the world, how do you raise a kid who is deeply committed to meeting the needs of other people sacrificially?

We live in a radically un-Christian society, with a value system that is practically the opposite of the one Jesus Christ set out in his Sermon on the Mount, but we seldom take that obvious fact into account when we think about the family in general. We make a big deal out of the things Jesus says about adultery and divorce, of course, and we teach our children to be honest and not to swear, but usually that's the extent of our practical applications.

As Americans, it violates our sense of patriotism to speak of not resisting evil or turning the other cheek, especially when we have a world to run. As responsible citizens who diligently save for a rainy day, it seems blasphemous to say, "Do not store up for yourselves treasures on earth," and irresponsible to say, "Do not worry about your life, what you will eat or drink, or your body, what you will wear." As Christian businessmen, we take issue with anyone who says, "You cannot serve both God and money."

The Beatitudes sound too passive, and we don't put much stock in persecution for the sake of righteousness because we are doing so well in this country. Besides, who would have the audacity to claim that anybody who says Jesus is Lord doesn't automatically go to Heaven, or that only a few people are ever going to find the road to eternal life? We know better than that sort of negative thinking in this country.

As a result, we have taken the commandments of Jesus and reworked them into a belief system that fits into our way of life instead of calling that way of life into question. Jesus said that the goal of life was to "Be perfect, therefore, as your heavenly Father is perfect" (Matthew 5:48). In modern-day America, however, we have a different credo to guide our lives: "Be happy." Happiness has become our new ultimate concern.

Perhaps it began with that famous phrase from the Declaration of Independence that describes the most basic human rights as "life, liberty, and the pursuit of happiness." Somehow, though, happiness has become the acceptable justification for everything from choosing a college to filing for divorce. People lose weight to be happy, quit jobs to be happy, and have sex to be happy. Incredibly enough, people get married to be happy. They even have kids to be happy. Once they have those kids, they do anything they can to make them happy, too. Their reasoning is simple. How can your kids make you happy if they aren't happy themselves?

It wasn't always this way, of course. People used to get married and have children, not to make themselves happy but in order to survive. In the farming societies of bygone years, the family was primarily an economic unit in which every member functioned as a valuable part of the labor force. Men and women had distinct roles and functions, and each needed the other to make things work. Furthermore, large families were normative because each successive child was an economic asset. People did not think in terms of *affording* their children—it was difficult to get along without them. Consequently, children of that era grew up with a genuine sense of value and purpose which grew directly out of their contributions to their families. If you asked a farmer near the turn of the century why he had kids, he probably would have matter-of-factly told you, "Because I need them."

Contrast that response with the reasons behind today's family, if you can find any. What exactly is the point of the family today? What is a family supposed to be? Why do people raise children in the first place?

I hesitate to ask those questions of you, Dad, because I'm afraid I might not like the answers. I know that you didn't need me in the way farmers needed kids years ago, but it is frightening for me to consider that I might have been conceived primarily for reasons of emotional gratification. Is a child's value and purpose in life really just to make his parents happy and to be happy himself? Is that really all there is to it?

The more I work with parents and kids the more I become convinced that happiness really is the primary motivation behind today's family. When I ask parents what they want their kids to do with their lives or what they want their kids to become, I inevitably get the same answer. "Oh, it doesn't matter to me what they do, as long as they're happy." In decisions about colleges, careers, friends, spouses, children, location—always the same criteria. "Whatever makes my daughter or son happy is all right with me." Families today are primarily based on the simple pursuit of happiness. Parents want their kids to be moral, healthy, well educated, hard working, and even Christian, but they want those things because they instinctively know that those things will ultimately lead to their kids' happiness, which is the parents' ultimate concern. That, I think, is the problem.

Happiness, you see, is a very elusive goal. Indeed, it seems like the more we try to make ourselves happy, the less happy we end up.

I remember going through a long period of depression one summer when I was seventeen years old. A girlfriend had broken off with me, I hated my summer job, and I had just had a car accident. All I did was mope around the house and watch television, and nothing anyone suggested to me sounded like the least bit of fun. I was sad, and I didn't know what to do about it. One day Mom came up to my room crying and sat down beside me. "Bart," she said, "I love you and it makes me so sad to see you this way. Just tell me what to do to make you happy, and I'll do it. All I want is for you to be happy again." A kind offer, to be sure, but her words only made me feel worse. I realized that my unhappiness was making her unhappy, and I felt pressured to find a way out of my depression—but I couldn't do it, Dad. Sometimes it is very hard thing to be happy.

Since then I think I've figured out why happiness is such an elusive goal. The reason is simple: you can only find happiness when you are looking for something else. Jesus said it this way: "Whoever finds his life will lose it, and whoever loses his life for my sake will find it" (Matthew 10:39). Our culture's preoccupation with happiness and personal fulfillment clearly has made us selfish people, but the worst part of it is that it hasn't made us happy. And it certainly hasn't produced a new generation of young people committed to serving the Kingdom of God.

In order to develop servant-hearted kids, parents must redefine their families, not as economic units, nor as happiness factories, but as missionary teams dedicated to Christian service. Perhaps that sounds radical, but stop and think about it for a moment.

If a modern family is an economic unit, dedicated to nothing more than achieving an ever-increasing level of wealth and material possessions, the kids in that family will see themselves as useless at best and very likely as liabilities as well. They do nothing to contribute to upward mobility, and actually slow their parents' progress toward a bigger and better house, car, wardrobe, and bank account. Marriage can be efficient, but children are bound to create problems for people on the fast track. Nobody with children actually looks at them that way, but in the absence of a clearly understood alternative goal, the kids are bound to figure out the obvious: the family is aimed at prosperity and they are just along for the ride. One of the most basic desires every person has is the desire to be important or necessary in some way. That isn't possible for kids in the family that is an economic unit. Those kids are bound to have some identity problems and are likely to become the kind of self-confident, compassionate young adults who will gravitate toward serving the Kingdom of God.

Exchanging economic prosperity for the more ambiguous goal of happiness doesn't help kids very much, either. As I've already said, happiness is a very elusive goal in the first place, and the pressure put on kids in whatever-makes-you-happy families makes things even worse. Furthermore, a family that puts happiness first simply cannot help but produce essentially selfish children. Happiness is a selfish goal. There must be a better way.

As far as I am concerned, that better way is to redefine the family as a missionary team. What that means is that parents who want their kids to become bona fide Christian disciples have to communicate by example and experience that following Jesus involves much more than personal salvation. I am not suggesting that kids don't need to learn the Good News of forgiveness and redemption through faith in Jesus Christ, but that is only the beginning. We must invite them to respond to the love and the grace of God.

We must introduce them to the vision of Philippians 2:1–5:

If you have any encouragement from being united with Christ, if any comfort from his love, if any fellowship with the Spirit, if any tenderness and compassion, then make my joy complete by being like-minded, having the same love, being one in spirit and purpose. Do nothing out of selfish ambition or vain conceit, but in humility consider others better than yourselves. Each of you should look not only to your own interests, but also to the interests of others. Your attitude should be the same as that of Christ Jesus.

What a tremendous passage for the Christian family! As followers of Christ, we are called not only to salvation, but to live our lives for God and to use all of our resources to do the work of his Kingdom. For a family that must mean more than just going to church or saying prayers before meals; it must become the spirit and purpose behind every action and decision.

A Christian family must look not only to its own members' prosperity or happiness, but also to the interests of others. That is where the love and unity that Paul writes about come from the shared sense of mission that grows out of the joy of being united with Christ.

Practically, I think, that means that every member of a Christian family needs to understand that the primary purpose of that family is not to achieve economic prosperity or even happiness, but to love and serve God and meet the needs of other people.

I know a family in Providence, Rhode Island, that is a perfect example of what I'm talking about: the Johns. I met them when I was a student at Brown, when I decided to volunteer as an assistant coach for an inner-city church basketball league. The head coach was Emil John, and every one of the players looked up to him as a father figure. He didn't just coach that team—he was personally involved with the life and family of every kid on it.

As I got to know Emil over the course of the year, I began to see that his ministry to our basketball team was only the beginning of his commitment to the church that sponsored it. Trinity United Methodist Church is located in a very rough part of Providence, surrounded by poverty, drugs, and crime. Emil has been there for more than twenty years, running everything from basketball leagues to an anti-drug club. But he is not the only one committed to ministry in that poor neighborhood. His wife runs a thrift shop there, and his daughter leads the Young Life Club for high-school kids. His sons coach the basketball teams along with Emil, and the whole family pitches in to help operate the L community theatre group that has grown up within the church. The Johns even run a soup kitchen on Sunday nights together with Emil's sister and her husband. Everywhere you look at Trinity, you see some of Emil's family working together to care for the needs of other people. His children are grown up, but their commitment to the Kingdom is tremendously strong, as is their commitment to their family. They are fun people to be with, too, full of the joy of the Lord and with a thousand stories to tell.

A kid growing up in a family like that has something only a common mission can provide; namely, the chance to participate as a full member. No longer are the parents the only ones who can make a contribution, for when the common purpose is to love and serve other people, even the youngest child can give something real. A little girl may not be able to earn a wage, but she becomes tremendously significant in an old folks home or at a hospital. Indeed, in that realm she may be more useful than her parents. A teenager may not be able to be happy on command, but he can serve food at the rescue mission and there develop a sense of meaning and importance.

Every family needs a "reason to be" outside of itself and its own well-being. Kids need to see in their parents' lives that life is a gift from God which he means for us to pass along. When a family begins to understand itself as a missionary team, it becomes a creative entity, with members always on the lookout for a lonely person in need of a home-cooked dinner with friends, or a neglected kid who would love to come along on an outing, or an old person who needs help cleaning the house. Kids develop a sense of compassion that offers their parents opportunities to help them discover how to express genuine love and understanding to people in need. Spiritual gifts and personal strengths assert themselves and can be encouraged and confirmed. Mutual love becomes mutual respect.

There is one more feature of the family that defines itself as a missionary unit that I think is especially important. It looks at wealth in the way Jesus looks at wealth: as a means of doing the work of the Kingdom rather than an end in itself. It amazes me to hear parents complain of their children's greed and ingratitude when I know that those parents have done nothing but encourage the notion that money is earned primarily to provide for personal needs and desires.

Materialism is a learned attitude, not part of our likeness to God. A family that claims its true purpose of serving God and raising him new servants is able to teach its children something else. Instead of materialism, the Christian family that is a missionary team will learn an attitude of stewardship that always asks the fateful question: "What would Jesus do with our money if it belonged to him?" This family knows the ultimate truth; their money does belong to him.

I have seen families give up their own gifts at Christmastime so that they could have the thrill of giving them to needy children—and I assure you that they didn't miss out on the joyful spirit of the holiday. On the contrary, they multiplied their blessings by living it out.

I have known families that made a game out of shopping at garage sales and thrift stores so they could use their savings to help a kid in their church go to college. It was fun for them to see who could find the best bargains, and even more fun to know that they were making a difference in the life of a friend.

When I worked in a meat-packing plant, I had a supervisor whose family lived well below its means in a smaller house and supported a foreign missionary all by itself. "We have a ministry together-with that guy in Africa," the man told me. "He needs us and we need him. I guess that means we are missionaries, too." What great logic—and what a great way for a family to develop young people who understand that everything in life is a gift from God that is meant to be given away all over again.

Of course, you can't force your kids to care about other people any more than you can force them to care about God. Sadly, all the redefining in the world cannot guarantee that a family will turn out servants of the Kingdom. Then again, I don't think God expects or requires that from parents in the first place.

People are born free, and that freedom is a gift from God that doesn't come with a "Do Not Open Until Age 18" card on top of it. Parents can do everything right, and their kids can still go wrong—and God the Father of us all knows that better than anyone. We have all gone wrong before him. Yet he loves us with a love so great that it overwhelms everything but itself. Again and again, he invites us to come back to him, to repent, to try again. He forgives us and he saves us, but he does even more than that. On top of everything else, God offers us the unbelievable privilege of participating in his ministry of reconciling the entire world to his love.

We have received the high calling of God in Christ Jesus, and that means that we not only have a new life, but a new purpose and meaning as well. We are not simply God's children—we are called to become his servants as well. There is work to be done. Being a full member of God's family requires a person to look beyond wealth or even happiness, to serving the Kingdom and meeting the needs of other people.

In a very real way, to be a full member of a Christian family requires the same thing. Individuals may eventually choose not to participate in a family that defines itself as a missionary unit, and at some point parents must allow that and understand that the freedom to do so is a gift of God. Yet in order for parents to communicate the full meaning of Christian discipleship to their children, they must understand the family as existing before God and be willing to say along with Joshua, "As for me and my household, we will serve the Lord" (Joshua 24:15).

I knew as a kid growing up that being part of our family meant standing for God and for the needs of poor people. I hope that one day my children will know the same thing, that it always means something to be a Campolo, the same way it means something to be part of the family of God. You gave me more than a happy childhood, Dad. You gave me a legacy. Like you, I may go through a lot of different stages, and God will probably change my direction a few times along the way. Nevertheless, I know what it means to be part of God's family, and that's the best place to start. I'll keep you posted.

Love,

Bart

NINE

DOING WHAT'S RIGHT WHEN YOU FEEL ALL WRONG

Dear Dad,

When I was in college, I saw a lot of kids who virtually ignored their parents except when they needed money. I often wondered how they could receive so much without feeling any obligation to the people who were giving it. As much as it bothered me, when my friends persistently avoided their parents' telephone calls and didn't bother to answer their letters, there was no way I could turn things around in my mind and blame those parents for failing to raise thoughtful kids. I couldn't do it because I knew that you and Mom had done a great job as parents, and yet I often failed and continue to fail to stay in touch with you and to let you in on my life the way that I should. I am just like the kids I knew in college. After all you've done for me, somehow I still tend to take you for granted.

I don't know exactly why it is that I don't call or write sometimes or why I don't come by when I know that there is some way I could help out around the house. It is fashionable these days for people to say that they are under a lot of pressure and that there simply isn't enough time, but I know better. It would be a lie to say that I'm too busy because no one is ever so busy that he can't make a five-minute phone call or send off a two-sentence postcard to say that things are all right or even that they're terrible, for that matter. My big sister Lisa (whom I am convinced has never failed in such matters) brought that point home to me once when I pleaded exam-week busy-ness after missing Mom's birthday. As you know, Lisa often isn't a very subtle person. She was angry and she let me know it.

"Did you watch any television last week—even for half an hour?" she demanded in a tone of voice that gave her away as a future lawyer. "Did you read the newspaper, or chat with your roommate, or play any basketball? Did you eat? Did you sleep?" She didn't wait for the answer. "Of course you did! So don't tell me there weren't five minutes you could have taken to send a measly birthday card to your own mother. The truth is that it just wasn't important enough to you, Bart. You didn't think about it—or her. And that, my dear boy, simply is not acceptable."

She was right, of course. I knew it then, and I know it now. But somehow I managed to convince myself that you and Mom would understand. You would take my thoughtlessness in stride, I reasoned, because in spite of everything I had failed to do, you knew that I really loved you. You knew that because I knew it, and because it was true, I told myself.

Yet as I look back on that lost birthday and all the other episodes like it, I realize that I was only kidding myself. Oh, you understood, all right, and you forgave me. But what you understood was that although I probably did love you, it was not very much and it certainly was not enough. I didn't see then that love only becomes real between people as it is expressed in action. Jesus said it best: "Greater love has no-one than this, that he lay down his life for his friends" (John 15:13).

Jesus did exactly that. His love for us was expressed in what he did for us—in coming to show us the truth about God's love, in dying for us so that we could enter into that love, and in rising from the dead so that we might do the same. To Jesus, love is not a collection of warm feelings toward the beloved, but a series of sacrificial actions on behalf of that person. That is why he is able to command us to love our enemies, because even though we cannot always control our emotions, we can in fact determine our actions because we are free.

Making sacrifices for other people is a free choice. The irony is that only when we do the actions that love requires will we really experience the feelings that love inspires. I didn't understand that love must express itself in sacrificial action, but I should have. I had you and Mom for parents.

Many of the young people to whom I speak fully expect their parents to provide not only the necessities of life but the luxuries as well. In the ghetto, of course, the situation is very different. Needy kids want the same things, but they don't expect to receive them. Rich or poor, however, I know a lot of parents who feel terribly guilty if they can't keep up with their kids' constant demands for new clothes, stereos, compact discs, skateboards, and whatever else happens to be in style at any particular moment.

We live in a tremendously materialistic culture, and kids growing up in the middle of it can't miss being affected. Everywhere they turn, there are messages telling them they have to have the right things or else they won't be acceptable or attractive to other people. Today when sixteen year olds say, "I need those jeans," they believe what they are saying. America has somehow convinced itself to measure people by what they look like and what they have, and that is bound to lead to greed.

Of course, sometimes the parents who complain loudest about their kids' greed are unhappy primarily because they themselves are already working overtime to finance their own desires for bigger and better cars, houses, boats, and furniture. I wonder how they can miss the obvious irony, and I don't enjoy being the one to point it out to them. Parents ought to expect no more from their kids than they do from themselves, in materialism as well as everything else.

It shocks me to see how much kids demand and expect from their folks—until I reflect on the way I always approached you when I was a kid. I never really thought about how whatever I was asking for translated into work or time for you. I perceived nearly all of it to be my birthright as your child. Even something as monumental as going away to college, I took for granted. I knew that everyone's parents couldn't afford such a thing, but I also knew that you and Mom could. And what you could do for me, I felt, you must do. Consequently, I never thought very much about the fact that you might have done otherwise, or about the sacrifices you were making, or about how indebted I was for all you provided. I had it coming.

I applied the what-you-can-do-for-me-you-must-do-for-me maxim to a lot more than just material things, of course. I came to expect you and Mom to see to it that my life went smoothly, no matter what I did or didn't do. When I decided to play Little League baseball, I didn't stop to consider how I would get there. Mom would drive or you would if you were home. When I came home late in the evening, I didn't wonder if I would get dinner. I just ate it. If I was sick, I stayed in bed until I felt better. I'm sure I saw Mom bringing in food and medicine, changing the sheets, and taking my temperature, but it never occurred to me that nursing me back to health was a labor of love, the same way those other things were. For years both of you bent over backwards in a million ways to make my life good, yet, for the most part, I figured that you had nothing better to do.

I'm sure that I thanked you once in a while, but that probably had more to do with wanting to keep a good thing going than with actual gratitude. Once again, I didn't perceive you as doing anything that wasn't your duty to me as my parents. It never occurred to me then that those sacrificial actions were the substance of your love for me.

Looking back, though, I cannot separate your love from the things you did because they are the same thing. That doesn't mean you bought me everything I wanted. I thank God that you didn't. That doesn't mean that every action was perfectly understood. Sometimes even the most sacrificial actions get misunderstood—like the time I hated my summer job, and you endured my endless complaints and whining without allowing me to quit. It would have been easier, I'm sure, just to give in and have been done with it, but you didn't, and I thought you were horrible for it at the time.

The fact that you did so much for me didn't mean that you didn't also have to say "I love you" or "You are special to me" over and over again. In matters of the heart, words are tremendously important, in the end, though, your love and Mom's love became real to me through what you did, consistently, day in and day out, as I was growing up. At the risk of being taken for granted, you made one thing crystal clear: I could count on you.

As I speak more and more to young people around the country, I am learning that most of them don't know anything at all about that kind of consistent love or about parents they can count on. These kids don't worry about taking their parents for granted because they have never had that chance. Instead, their parents are the focus of their lives precisely because their parents can *never* be counted on.

It is difficult for me to write about the kids who have suffered at the hands of their own parents. I worry that some of the people who read these letters are going to be deeply hurt by some of the things we describe or suggest because their families are so different from ours. I want those people to know that you and I care very deeply about their lives. There is nothing in the world that is more devastating than a destructive family, and if someone is in that situation, I pray that they will not despair as they read this letter, but will instead turn to someone trustworthy for help. Unfortunately, many people who have been hurt or are being hurt by their families don't realize that they need help, or even that such help is available to them.

Sally was fifteen years old when she confided in me that her father had forced her to have sexual relations with him from the time she was ten until she was fourteen. I would never have guessed her problem by looking at her happy-go-lucky appearance. On the inside, Sally was full of pain, anger, embarrassment, confusion, and guilt. Like so many victims of sexual abuse, she was certain that she had done something wrong to deserve her horrible fate. She hated what had happened to her, but she felt completely alone and helpless. After she heard me talk about sexual abuse in a sermon, she found the courage to pull me aside and ask for help.

I am not a trained counselor, but I was able to listen to her, support her, and pray for her as she told me her story. Later on, I was able to put her in touch with a friend of mine who works with victims of sexual abuse. My friend is not only a well-trained professional, she is also a survivor herself, and living proof that restoration can happen. For the first time since her ordeal began, Sally could see some hope for healing in her life. I did my best to help her establish a relationship with Jesus Christ because I knew that she would need the love of God and the strength of the Holy Spirit as she struggled to piece her broken life back together. I left Sally with the best things I had to offer, but as I got on the plane to fly home after talking with her, I still felt helpless and upset. I wanted to find the man who had hurt her and beat him up, both to punish him and to keep him from hurting anyone else that way. How could he have betrayed his own daughter that way? How could anyone abuse his own child?

Sexual abuse is not as uncommon as we would like to think, Dad. One out of every three girls and one out of every eight boys in this country are sexually abused before they reach the age of eighteen, and most of that abuse comes from family members. Beatings and physical abuse are also common occurrences for many more kids than we know of, and that doesn't begin to touch on the millions of people who are not sexually abused or beaten but are still denied the consistent love of a parent they can count on. It is difficult to know which is more prevalent—abuse or neglect. These are serious subjects, Dad, and I don't pretend to be an expert on how to deal with them. What I do know is that when someone is in a destructive family situation, it must be stopped and dealt with. If anyone reading these letters is in trouble themselves, or knows someone who is, I hope that he or she will get professional help and turn to a trustworthy Christian supporter so that God can be a part of the healing as well.

I was fortunate in that I never had to worry about being abused, and that's a big part of the reason I can reflect on my childhood so easily. But that is not enough. To be able to count on your parents means more than not having to worry about being hurt, and more even than not having to worry about their love for you. It means not having to worry about whether or not your parents will stay together.

I guess there was a time when divorce was a big deal in this country, but it must have been before I was around. By the time I was graduated from high school, at least half of my classmates' families had broken up. As kids, we didn't talk about it very much among ourselves, but we always knew when someone's parents were divorcing. We didn't talk, I think, because there was nothing we could say that would change anything. Divorce was—and is—a fact of life.

I know a lot more about marriage and divorce now that I am grown up and have a wife myself, but when I meet a kid whose parents are splitting up, I still don't always know what to say. In a way, I feel like I have no right to say anything. You and Mom never gave me any reason to think about divorces except as they related to other people. Whatever else might happen, I always knew that you would stay together, the same way I knew that school would always open in September and that Lisa would always be smarter than I was. You don't think about things like that—they just are.

So what can I say to someone who is wondering all the time what is going to happen to her family? That I'm sorry? Of course, I'm sorry. That never seems like enough. I don't want to belabor this because I am writing to you, and you never let it be an issue, but I will say this: if parents get divorced because they want to be happy or free or fulfilled or any of that when they could have tried harder to make things work, they are selfish people and their kids will surely suffer. When people have affairs, they are shafting their kids for their own pleasure. When wives and husbands let their marriages become battle-fields because they are unwilling to make sacrifices, they don't love their kids, no matter what they say, because love is made of sacrificial actions.

I know you love Mom, Dad, and I know she loves you, too, but I'm old enough now to know that there were times when one or both of you felt like walking out. I know you had opportunities for affairs with other women because I traveled with you. I know there were struggles. You and Mom worked hard to make things look good to me. It was your sacrifice to make sure I never had to worry, that I could always count on both of you—together. You handled my need for security the same way you did all those other things. You were consistent with your love. I depended on you without ever really thinking about it, and you didn't let me down. You were by no means perfect parents, but your love was always there, in the million sacrificial actions that were the foundation of my childhood.

All of that is why the fact that I have often failed to be sacrificial where you and Mom are concerned bothers me. Of course, the sacrifices I owe you are different from the ones you made for me because you don't have to depend on me the way I had to depend on you. As I sit here trying to figure out just what those sacrifices are, I can't help but compare my relationship with you and Mom to my relationship with my Father in heaven. These are similar relationships in a lot of ways, although less so as I grow older because, although I am no longer primarily dependent on you, I am still completely a child before him. The love he wants from me now is the same as the love you wanted from me when I was a kid: obedience—"If you love me, you will obey what I command," Jesus says to his disciples (John 14:15), and I hear echoes of your voice in my ears.

You have always commented with pride that I was a pretty easy kid to raise as far as obedience went, but I must finally admit that the biggest reason for that had nothing to do with being afraid of what you would do to me if I challenged your authority. Honestly, fear was seldom a significant factor. I just never have liked conflict. Usually, following even your most ridiculous commands was preferable to the arguments and lectures that came along with disobedience. Eventually I came to realize that in obeying you I was giving you the one thing you most wanted from me—I was loving you, really—and I began to get a kick out of making you happy that way. Of course, making you happy tended to work in my favor, too, but that's the way it usually works in matters of love. What you are giving and what you are getting become blurred in the joy of it all.

When I tell kids that obedience is the key to dealing with their parents, they usually think I am being naïve. "It's not that simple," they tell me, and yet so often when we take the problems those kids are having with their parents and break them down into their basic elements, it's just that simple.

A child's obedience to his parents must gradually and inevitably give way to another kind of love. In the end, God is the only authority, and we all stand equal before him alone. In the words of a wise man, "The ground is level at the Cross." Consequently, the sacrificial things I can do for you as a Christian adult must be different from those I did for you as a child. I am my own person now. I can't keep following your commands. Happily, there is something else I can do for you, Dad.

As I think about the things I have done and even more about the things that I have failed to do—I see clearly that inasmuch as I have loved you effectively, my actions have moved from obedience to involvement. As far as I can figure it out, that is what you want most from me now. I don't know when the shift began—I suspect it was before I even got to junior high—but somewhere along the line I realized that, from your perspective, loving you meant letting you in on my life. Like most parents, you didn't want to be left in the dark.

I am a big part of your life, and it matters to you that we stay connected and that you are a big part of my life, too. That's what Lisa was trying to tell me when she yelled at me about missing Mom's birthday. That is why it hurts you when I don't send a postcard or make a phone call. You want to be involved. This is the place where I have failed so often and where I sense I have hurt you the most. The worst of it is that I know what I should do. I tell kids about it all the time.

"Ask your parents for advice when you can," I say, "because they love to be a part of your thinking as you figure things out. You don't have to follow it always, but just asking them lets them know what's going on in your life. Invite your mom out to dinner some night, just the two of you, and ask her about herself the way you would a real date. Or your dad, maybe. Or set aside half an hour each week when you turn off everything else and pick a topic like friendship or travel or music to talk about with either one of them. They'll love it."

I think I have the most advice for college students because that is where I failed so much. I tell them to send their mom the school newspaper once in a while, a graded paper (so long as it's a decent grade), or a copy of their class schedule. I tell them to call, even for five minutes, at the same time every week so their folks can look forward to it all week long. I tell them to stamp and address twenty postcards all at once and send two a week, because it's the biggest return they will ever get on fifteen cents. "It takes a minute and a half for you, but it makes your folks' entire week," I tell them. I say all the right stuff . . . and then I forget to do it myself.

To some people, those may seem like little things. Those little things, however, let your parents in on your thoughts and decisions and everyday life, and they are the sacrificial actions of love. When love is communicated, when it is expressed in action, it becomes real in a wonderful way.

This is the risk you and Mom run: being taken for granted. You've been as reliable as a good wristwatch, and as a result, I've had the privilege of concentrating on other things, secure in the knowledge that I am loved.

If that has meant that I have failed to love you back the way I should have, it is my own fault for not learning the lessons of love better. Believe me, Dad, I don't want it to be that way. I love you. I want you to know that, the same way that I know you love me. I want you to be able to count on me, too.

Maybe there's something I'm leaving out, though, something you really want from me that I don't even know about. I know you pretty well, but I can't read minds and I have no idea what it is like to be where you are in life. No kid ever knows that kind of thing. In fact, I would consider it a great favor if you would tell me straight out what it is that you want from me, especially as you get older, so I can know that I'm loving you the best way I can. Sometimes people just don't know what to do for each other without being told. I can't promise you I will be able to manage everything you want all the time, but I will try my best to love you—the real way—for as long as we are both alive.

Love,

Bart

*   *   *   *

Dear Bart,

If you have learned that love is something you do, you have learned the most important of all lessons. The Bible makes this truth abundantly clear, but all too few grasp its message. All the way though the Scriptures, love is seen as action that lies within the prerogatives of the will. Love, is not something we effortlessly feel, as is so commonly assumed in our romanticized culture. Instead, it is that which we are commanded to do. The Bible says to love the Lord your God, to love your neighbor, to love your wife, and even to love your enemies. Now on that last one, people who instinctively feel positive emotions for those who hurt or humiliate them are strange. People who treat others as Jesus would want them treated, even when they don't feel like doing so, are lovers in the biblical sense.

Love, is really impossible to define, although the Apostle Paul does as good a job as can be done in his brilliant thirteenth chapter of 1 Corinthians. My own working definition is simply this: love is a decision to do for the other person what Jesus would do for that person if he were in your place. I do not want to suggest that feelings are not involved in biblically prescribed love—in reality, there are deep and gratifying feelings connected with it. These fulfilling feelings, however, come as a result of doing. You cannot count on your feelings to make you do the right thing, but those who choose to do what love requires eventually come to know a sense of inner joy and spiritual gratification that is what life at its best is all about. You said much the same thing in your letter to me.

Love, doesn't always give us the kinds of peak experiences that romantic turn-ons provide—but then the pleasure of romance is only fleeting, while love is everlasting. What love at its best really does is to lift us up to a higher plateau of living. A wonderful old hymn refers to this as "higher ground." Love, creates a new kind of humanity and lifts people up to a new kind of ongoing existence. Romance can never be trusted, but love is always there when you need it.

I have long been impatient with married men who claim to love their wives but treat them like dirt. In one particular case, a guy who had constantly been unfaithful to his wife sat with her in my office and tried to tell me that, in spite of everything, he really loved her. This guy had not even been kind to her when he was with her. He had ridiculed her in front of other people. He never did anything to make her life easier or better. Yet there he was, sitting across from me, saying in cavalier fashion that he really loved her. I figured that he wanted me to smile benevolently and say, "Poor Harry. He really is a loving guy. He just has some bad manners and personality weaknesses."

If old Harry was expecting something like that, he must have been shocked when I shot back at him, "You don't love her at all. Maybe she turns you on every now and then. Maybe you enjoy the acceptance she provides when you don't deserve it. Maybe you're afraid to face life without her mothering influence, but don't tell me you love her. Love, is doing what Jesus would want done for her. Love, is responding to her needs and providing whatever would help her to experience the life that Jesus wants for her. I don't see any of that in you. Tell me that you need her to exploit for your own ego purposes. Tell me that you have some kind of sickness that drives you to hurt a person who is loyal to you, but don't tell me that you love her and then go on doing what you've been doing."

This turned out to be one of my more successful counseling cases. That man came to the realization that he had to stop playing games and face the reality of the true nature of love. In the end, love meant that he had to make a decision to change—and he did. The marriage was saved.

In your relationship with Mom and me, you loved us enough to change. It took a while, but you got the message about what love required, and you began to do the things that express love and that generate those gratifying feelings that give life luster. You do make those caring telephone calls these days. You often remember your special people with notes. Yes, you still occasionally forget birthdays, but your overall pattern is one of concern, and you are doing better with every passing day. Love, involves being willing to change, and in many ways you have heeded that call. Mom and I are proud of you. You have worked hard on something that did not come easy to you. Love, is being willing to listen, and you have always seemed to love Mom and me enough to listen to us. If there were something important or difficult to tell you, we could always be sure that you would pay serious attention to what we had to say. If there were suggestions we wanted to make about how you could improve as a person, you could be counted on to listen. If we saw you moving in directions that we felt could be hurtful to others or harmful to yourself, you were willing to think about what we had to say. You didn't always yield to our directions, but you made us feel that you would give careful consideration to our viewpoints and proposals. Mom and I always felt that you heard us when we had something important to say to you. That is love.

I want you to know that we have not taken this for granted.

Love,

Dad

TEN

FIGURING OUT WHAT REALLY MATTERS

Dear Bart,

Balancing was one of my most difficult struggles. How to reconcile the time demands of my career, on the one hand, with the need to spend time with you and Lisa, on the other, had me constantly straining for answers. How to give the best possible effort to my work and, at the same time, be a good father and husband kept me constantly perplexed. I think that many middle-class types like me have the same problem, and the way in which we handle it is one of life's most important ethical concerns.

I talked recently with a young married couple. The husband is a really great Christian guy, but he is not handling this problem of balancing well at all. He is very involved in missionary service and is the driving force behind an incredible work for God. His ministry has him on the road constantly. He is not paying much attention to his wife or his two sons. His wife loves him and thinks that what he is doing is wonderful, but she, nevertheless, feels neglected. She has silently and sadly resigned herself to a kind of married life that has left her lonely and disappointed. She has figured out how to make the best of her lot, and she is doing quite well, considering the overall situation. This young woman has learned to live with the hurt that goes with the awareness that her husband's work is his primary concern and that she must settle for whatever time is left over. Something inside her is dying, and I hope that this guy doesn't wake up too late to see what he is doing to her.

I did my best to tell him how I saw his situation, but I had the feeling that he didn't intend to be the one doing any adjusting.

This particular man has also neglected his two boys, who are seven and fourteen, like their mother, the boys think that their dad is the neatest thing that ever came down the pike. But also like their mom, they sense that they are not very important in the grand scheme of things as far as their father is concerned.

This man knows better, but he can come up with a thousand justifications as to why he doesn't have more time for his family. Because his work is so noble, his wife and kids are made to feel guilty if they ever suggest that he do less of it and give more time to them. He's not balancing well at all.

I feel a particular pain as I listen to this good guy who is doing such a wrong and stupid thing. The reason I am so pained by his lifestyle is that I know that I may have been guilty of the same thing during your growing-up years. Did I balance things right? Did I divide my time in a way that left you, Mom, and Lisa knowing that you were always the most important persons in my life? I can't help but wonder . . .

In retrospect, I know I failed to take the biblical concept of the Sabbath seriously. The Bible teaches that one day each week should be set aside from all labor and should be spent with the family in spiritual renewal. Every family, according to the teachings of Scripture, should have a day each week to nurture relationships with one another and with the Lord. If Sunday is a workday, which it always has been for me, then another day should be set aside for this purpose. The particular day of the week that is observed as the Sabbath is not what is important; what is important is that we recognize that our observing such a day is a commandment of God.

If I had it to do over again, I would make one day a week a family day and have us all spend it together doing something fun and special. Doing that would have enabled me to balance life better and to be a better father.

The problem of balancing is as old as the church itself. The Apostle Paul, way back in the first century, recognized that this was a primary problem for married Christians. He saw that there was an inevitable conflict between the time and energy required to do the work of building God's kingdom and the time and energy required to be a good spouse and parent. He wrote of that dilemma in 1 Corinthians without ever resolving for us how it should be resolved.

> He that is unmarried careth for the things that belong to the Lord, how he may please the Lord: But he that is married careth for the things that are of the world, how he may please his wife.
> *1 Corinthians 7:32–33*

In that same chapter, however, Paul urges Christians who are married to pay proper attention to one another lest they become ready bait for extramarital messing around.

> Defraud ye not one the other, except it be with consent for a time, that ye may give yourselves to fasting and prayer; and come together again, that Satan tempt you not for your incontinency. But I speak this by permission, and not of commandment.
> *1 Corinthians 7:5–6*

Paul says in verse 7 that concessions must be made when people are married in order to nurture relationships and, therefore, that it is impossible to be totally committed to do the work of one's Christian vocation and be married at the same time. On the one hand, it surely can be argued that being a father and husband makes a Christian in ministry more understanding of the situations that are normative in most people's lives. On the other hand, there is no doubt that for most ministers there is an unbearable tension between the call to faithfulness to the work of the church and the call to fulfill the obligations that go with being a good spouse and parent. This balancing act is difficult, and most of us drop the ball somewhere along the line.

I have often heard the problems of balancing time allotments discussed at ministerial get-togethers. Regularly I have heard ministers and missionaries say with regret that they wished they had spent more time with their families and less time on their ministries. *Never once have I heard a minister say that he wished that he had spent less time with his family and more time on the work of the church.* That should tell us all a thing or two.

This problem of balancing may be even more of a problem for those in so-called secular vocations. People who work in offices or factories can find themselves torn apart in even more painful ways than those in religious work. Besides the conflict that exists between the time demands of work and family, these people are likely to find themselves condemned from the pulpit if they do not get involved in the programs of their local church. It's bad enough for a young husband to have to try to figure out what he should be doing about balancing the time demands of his career over against the time demands of his family, but then, on top of all that, he finds the preacher stepping in and laying a guilt trip on him if he isn't giving "sufficient" time to all the things that the church has for him to do. Preachers can be very unsympathetic to the man who puts his family time before the Thursday night men's fellowship meeting or the Tuesday evening door-to-door evangelism program.

If family life is as important to the Christian church as its leaders say it is, there should be more care exercised in what those leaders ask of people, lest they exhaust the time that families need for togetherness. Perhaps churches need to plan more intergenerational programs or projects in which a family could participate as a group. Certainly, the church should not be making it more difficult for men to be decent fathers and husbands.

Finding time for you always required that I be extremely creative. For instance, when my teaching load and graduate studies tied up my afternoons and evenings, I tried to compensate by spending time with you in the very early morning. Remember when we would get up at 6:00 a.m. and go out to the soccer field to kick the ball around for an hour or so? I still remember you standing at my bedside, all dressed in your soccer outfit, holding the ball in your hands and saying in your soft, eight-year-old voice, "Dad. It's time."

We would go out to the soccer field with only our dog, Lady, to watch. We would run up and down the field, yelling and screaming as we kicked the ball. Lady would follow, jumping and barking as she played with us. I never pass by that soccer field without remembering the good times we had there.

Another way that I made time to be with you was by includ-ing you in what I was doing. When you were just seven years old, I started taking you with me on weekend speaking engagements. Those were quality times. We had long one-on-one discussions about almost everything. Those trips meant so much to me that I've encouraged friends of mine, whose work also requires a lot of travel, to take their children along with them. You and I had especially good times on trips that required airplane flights, when we had nobody to talk to but each other. We explored cities together. We discussed the ways of the world and the customs of their kinds of people. We learned a lot about each other on those weekend trips. I was filled with sadness when our traveling days came to an end. When you got into your teens, you had your own life to live with ball practice and school activities. Like Puff the Magic Dragon, I suffered a bit when my little Jackie Paper wasn't around to play with me. I often wish I could relive those spe-cial times that we had together. I don't know why everybody whose work requires travel doesn't try to do what we did. It helped me do my balancing act.

Breakfast was always an important time with our family. Because my work often kept me from being home for supper, we made breakfast a time of special sharing. Mom went out of her way to cook up great food to start off each day, and all of us enjoyed the give and take in conversation as we sat around the table. Not only did I enjoy this time with my family, but my sociological studies at the university provided me with ample evidence that having meaningful discussions while eating together can be an essential component of the healthy social-ization of children. Around the table, values can be communi-cated and meal times allow parents time for helping kids to evaluate life in the light of the Scriptures. Table talk is more likely to be remembered than any lectures parents may give to kids.

I believe that table talk should be planned to include signif-icant topics. It was often during our breakfast hours that I tried to tell you about Christ's bias toward the poor and oppressed. It was around the table that we discussed the pros and cons of the arms race. I did my best to make our talks at breakfast important times of sharing as well as educational. Even as I write this, I especially recall an in-depth discussion we had one morning on interracial marriage.

A couple of students at Eastern College (whom you especially liked) were planning to get married, and there was some deplorable gossip going around the campus because he was black and she was white. As we talked about this upcoming marriage, I made sure that you clearly understood that there was nothing unbiblical about interracial marriage. Furthermore, in that conversation, I also had the chance to teach you that while the Bible does not prohibit interracial marriage, it does have some very specific teachings against Christians marrying non-Christians. I think the message stuck. You ended up marrying a wonderful committed Christian.

One of the most important ways to maintain balance in the midst of the topsy-turvy world in which most young fathers have to live is through family rituals. Rituals are prescribed ways of doing certain things, like putting kids to bed, eating, or celebrating special days like birthdays and holidays. Tevye, in the musical *Fiddler on the Roof*, referred to them as "traditions." Since the great Emile Durkheim, sociologists have called them "collective rituals."

Rituals have a variety of important functions. They build family solidarity and intensify the loyalty of family members to one another. They give children a sense of order about life, and this in turn contributes greatly to their emotional stability. Rituals are excellent ways for teaching children the vital things about life and helping them remember what must never be forgotten.

Family rituals were important around the Campolo home. Special days were always celebrated with great fanfare. On birthdays, we always made a fuss with birthday cakes and parties. Holidays like Christmas and Thanksgiving were always planned to follow an established pattern.

Mom was particularly good at rituals. She would put you to bed with an array of them that must have instilled in you a happy attitude of expectation about life. Every night, she would tell you special stories she made up about an incredible boy named Billy Anthony. Of course, we all knew that Billy Anthony was a thinly veiled, blown-up portrayal of you.

In Mom's stories, Billy Anthony was a wonder boy who could drive any kind of vehicle and was willing to perform all kinds of heroic feats to rescue people who were in trouble. I wonder if you've reflected much upon how important Mom's stories were in your character formation. I am convinced that the ritualistic day-in and day-out telling of those stories helped to build into your psyche the expectation that your life should be spent in service to others. I also believe that those stories taught you that, when difficulties arose in the course of helping others, you could prevail by facing them with self-confidence and assurance.

I often wonder why most parents don't recognize how important it is to give their kids a sense of well-ordered stability through rituals. As far as I'm concerned, life has become far too spontaneous for children in today's world. Most of them suffer emotionally because they don't know what to expect in their daily round of activities. Rituals, those expected routines in our lives, are essential to being civilized. Too many kids are denied them.

For fathers who are involved in careers that have them coming and going, rituals are of utmost importance. Family rituals can be what make such fathers put the demands of family life above the demands of their jobs. Too often, professionals live their own lives and expect their families to adapt to their schedules of activities. Rituals can correct this tendency and force fathers to realize that there are important events and ceremonies connected with their families for which business schedules must be sacrificed. Rituals can help fathers organize their lives around celebrations and observances that belong to the family, and this can keep them from becoming unbalanced workers, swallowed up by the time demands of their work.

Balancing is not only a matter of time, it is also a matter of values. Judgments and decisions have to be made in the course of every life and, in making these day-by-day judgments and decisions, people reveal what really matters to them.

One particular decision, more than any other, forced me to weigh what was good for my career over against what was good for you. When the weighing task was over, it was clear that if I did what was best for my career, the price would be too high in terms of your well-being.

As you were entering your junior year of high school, I had a chance to become the president of a small Christian college in New England. I really wanted that position, and I think I could have done some good for the Kingdom had I taken it. Mom and I talked it over and recognized that the consequences of uprooting you would be unpredictable. You were happy in your school, you were having a good time at church, and you had a great network of Christian friends. Even though you told me that you were willing to make the move, we felt that we owed it to you to let you enjoy having roots. Too often, as far as I'm concerned, parents allow the demands of their vocations to take precedence over the well-being of their kids and make moves that cause their children upset and pain. Mom and I were fortunate in being able to choose, and we chose not to take the risk. I knew that there would be other chances for me to live out my vocational dreams and visions, but I had only one chance to raise my son.

Your time to make hard decisions is at hand, Bart. You are a married man with a wife who deserves time. You are also starting out in a career of Christian service that demands time. Here's hoping you do well in the most important balancing act of your life.

Love,

Dad

*   *   *   *

Dear Dad,

I don't know how to say this except just to come out and say it: I wish we had spent more time together when I was growing up. I don't want you to feel guilty or bad, because it wasn't all your fault. You were trying to balance your family with your career and your service for God. I was intent on my friends, my sports, occasionally my studies, and, when I got old enough, girls. Somehow we both got busy, and the time got away from us. Not always, but too often.

You worked too much. I didn't invite you to be part of what I was doing often enough. It wasn't until I dropped out of college that we realized we were down to our last chance to really be together. We made the most of that year, and to me it was the best year we ever had. That was when we got close and finally figured out who each other really was. It was great having enough time to do it.

I feel sorry for that man that you counseled who was so busy trying to save the world that he had no time for his kids. The world will always be there, but his kids won't. There really is such a thing as too late. It makes me feel even worse to know that he's sacrificing his relationships with his wife and kids in the name of Christian ministry, because I know the kind of frustration that will cause for them.

It's one thing to resent your dad's business or his hobbies or his adult friends, but how do you resent his working for Jesus without feeling bad and selfish? How do you compete with God? How can a Little League game or an afternoon walk or a few hours together baking cookies stand up against what your dad says is his opportunity and obligation to do something important for the Kingdom? Those kids may even grow to hate God for stealing their father from them, the way they might hate another woman or alcohol, but they'll have a hard time admitting that, even to themselves, because they probably know it isn't right to hate God. Their father has probably taught them that much.

God isn't really stealing their father, of course; ambition or workaholism or a mixed-up set of priorities are, but those kids may not understand that for a long time. You are probably wondering if that's how I felt. Sometimes. But not often, Dad, because you did take me with you. You let me be a part of your life away from home. I must admit that when I see your schedule now, I'm glad you weren't such a big shot back when I was a kid.

Why do I wish we had spent more time together? You managed well enough to keep me from resenting your career. You entertained at my birthday parties. You came to my games. You and Mom created rituals that gave me a sense of security and belonging. Why do I think you should have been around more if I didn't miss you back then? It's simple, Dad. Because I miss you now.

I'm twenty-six years old. I have a wife, a career, and a life of my own. My childhood is gone now, and I can't do a thing about it. A few years ago, they tore down my elementary school to put up an office building. The other night, I ran into Robin Roach, who was the first girl I ever kissed, back when we were in seventh grade, and I felt so old when she told me she was a senior analyst for a major corporation. There's a parking lot now in the field where my friends and I used to camp out. I'm losing my hair. Everything that was a part of my childhood is slipping away into time and all that is left of it for me to hold onto is a bunch of old photographs and my memories.

Who I am is all caught up with those special things that happened when I was a kid, and I think about them a lot these days. It wasn't very hard for me to come up with the stories in these letters, Dad. They are the stories I tell all the time when I'm trying to explain who I am or what I think or how I feel about something.

Some of the stories are sad, and some of the memories are painful, but most of them are a joy to recall. Over the years, though, all of those images of growing up have sorted themselves out inside me, according to their relative importance. A million hours of television are forgotten, but the twenty minutes I watched the great Karl Wallenda walk the tightrope over Veteran's Stadium are as fresh in my mind now as if they were yesterday and not fifteen years ago. I spent a lot of my childhood with my buddy, John Baxter, and we can sit for hours and talk about every model airplane and every argument we ever had. Not much about school, mind you, just the things that mattered to us as boys. I played in a lot of soccer games, but the state championship game is the only one that I still know by heart, the only one that means something to me even now.

I cherish that game like a treasure because, even in defeat, my team and I played with all our hearts and we were proud. I dream sometimes about blocking the shot that beat us, but it doesn't bother me anymore that we lost. It was enough to have had the experience.

The times that I remember best, though, are the times I spent with you. I love those memories best of all, Dad, and they're a big part of who I am. That's the whole point of these letters for me. My childhood is gone, and I will never be able to be with you the way I was with you as a little boy. I will never be that small, and you will never seem that big again. But I have my stories, and they comfort me when I am overwhelmed by the world, when I am too old all of a sudden, when I lose my sense of wonder. They are all I have of my boyhood, and the reason I wish we had spent more time together is that I wish I had more of them now. It isn't that you didn't do enough, you see, for I would always want more. You were the king of the world back then, the imp of fun, the man with all the answers, the one who could always fix what was broken. You made life seem magical to me.

When you die, Dad, I will surely go to pieces for a while, because I still count on you more than anyone knows, but in the end I will be all right. I will have my stories, and in them I will always have part of you, the part that tells me who I am and where I came from. I only wish there was more because what there is means the world to me.

Love,

Bart

AFTERWORD

This is a very personal book. There are a lot of ideas and suggestions in it that I hope will be of some help to people, but essentially it is a story—our story. That is not what my father and I intended for it to be when we began, but that is what it became. To be honest, I am a bit uncomfortable putting our relationship out in front of people, but I am also hopeful that good will come of it.

The problem with any story, though, is that while it may be true, it is never altogether factual. Our perceptions of things are always conditioned by who we are. When a person says, "this is what happened," what we should hear is, "this is what I saw," or "this is what *I* experienced." Only God knows what really happened.

Our family understands that better than most because we love stories more than practically anything else. We tell them all the time, in sermons and around the kitchen table. Sometimes, at the end of a really good story, one of us will ask, "Did it really happen that way?" to which the standard family answer is always, "Well, if it didn't, it should have."

Maybe that is why I am a bit uncomfortable with putting my upbringing at center stage, because I don't want it to seem like my father and I are bragging about ourselves or one another or that our relationship is nothing less than a series of perfect illustrations. The stories in this book really happened. I know—I was there. Inasmuch as they are true, they are also our memories, and sometimes we wrote what we heard instead of what somebody else really said. I love movies where people say just the right thing at just the right time, but I know better than to expect real life to work that way. In real life you don't get to rehearse your lines.

If it looks as though my parents are the most absolutely wonderful people in the world, well, that's just the way it is as far as I am concerned. If it seems as though our lives are something out of a storybook, remember that that is exactly what you have here.

Bart Campolo

YOU CAN MAKE A DIFFERENCE

Tony Campolo

Young people, you're thinking the world's too big and we can't change it. We CAN change it!

With his incomparable blend of humor and biblical insight, Tony challenges young people on the following topics:

Commitment: "When you become a Christian, Jesus will invade your life and make you into somebody he can use to change the world. He wants to use you to touch the lives of people who are hurt, to bring joy to people who are sad. He wants to make you into an agent fighting for his great revolution."

Vocation: "Believe me, there is nothing you can do with your life that will make you happier than giving it away to others for Jesus."

Boyfriends and girlfriends: "I am calling upon you to surrender your life to Jesus. This requires that you order your boyfriends or girlfriends, your sex life, marriage or state of singleness in accordance with his will."

Discipleship: "There is a tremendous loss of people who make a decision for Jesus Christ, but who do not follow it through. I hope that you will give careful attention to these biblically prescribed instructions which I believe to be essential for the maintenance of the Christian life."